THE BUTT-FILES

BEAVIS & BUTT-HEAD'S GUIDE TO SCI-FI AND THE UNKNOWN

CREATED BY MIKE JUDGE
WRITTEN BY GREG GRABIANSKI AND AIMEE KEILLOR

books

MTV BOOKS / POCKET BOOKS

UHH, I'D LIKE TO DEADIKATE THIS BOOK TO MY BUTT, HUH-HUH-HUH-HUH! YEAH, HEH-HEH-HEH, UMM, I'D LIKE TO DEFICATE THIS BOOK TO MY NADS, HEH-HEH-HEH. WITHOUT WHO I'D, UMM, HAVE NO NADS, HEH-HEH-HEH-HEH.

Beavis and Butt-head are not role models. They're not even human. They're cartoons.
Some of the things they do would cause a real person to get hurt, expelled, arrested, possibly deported.
To put it another way: don't try this at home.

Beavis and Butt-Head created by Mike Judge
Written by: Greg Grabianski and Aimee Keillor
Edited by: Kristofor Brown
Art Direction: Roger Gorman/Leah Sherman, Reiner, NYC
Senior Art Supervisor: Dominie Mahl
Art Supervisor: Sharon Fitzgerald
Production Coordinator: Sara Duffy
Illustrators: Mike Judge, John Allemand, Karen Disher, Bryon Moore, Mike Baez
Ink and Paint: Monica Smith, Lisa Klein
Background Painters: Bill Long, Sophie Kittredge
Additional Illustrators: Brad MacDonald, Willy Hartland, Eugene Salandra
Production Assistants: James Wood, Tati Nguyen, Matt LaBarge

Special Thanks: John Andrews, Christine Friebely, Andrea Labate, Ed Paparo, Renee Presser, Robin Silverman, Donald Silvey, Abby Terkuhle, and Van Toffler.

Special thanks at Pocket Books to: Lynda Castillo, Gina Centrello, Kendra Falkenstein, Max Greenhut, Felice Javit, Eric Rayman, Dave Stern, Kara Welsh, and Irene Yuss. Also thanks to Al Travison at Stevenson, and Paula Trotto.

An Original Publication of MTV Books/Pocket Books

POCKET BOOKS, a division of Simon and Schuster, Inc.
1230 Avenue of the Americas, New York NY 10020

Photo credits: AP/World Wide Photo p. 5, 24, 62, 76; Archive Photos p. 7, 20, 24, 44, 71, 76, 84, 85;
Everett Collection p. 9, 13, 24, 30, 38, 41, 49, 54, 57, 74, 76, 84, 85, 92; Photofest p. 18, 24, 29, 50, 57, 66;
Bettmann p. 49; Orbital Media Ltd. p. 42; Jerry Ohlingers's p. 49, 71, 81, 83;
Retna Ltd. p. 91; FPG International p. 91.

ISBN: 0-671-01426-9

First MTV Books/Pocket Books trade paperback printing August 1997

10 9 8 7 6 5 4 3 2 1

Printed in the U.S.A.

INTRODUKSHUN

So it's, like, me and Beavis keep seeing all these movies and TV shows about the suppernatural and the unknown and stuff. Where dudes are like, "Uhh, this is a mystery. Nobody can explain it! It is beyond all human comprehension!" Huh-huh-huh! Dumb-asses! It's like, they can't explain this stuff 'cause they're, you know, stupid or something. Huh-huh-huh!

Heh-heh-heh! Yeah! Stupid buttholes! Heh-heh!

So we, like, checked out a bunch of this suppernatural and unknown crap for ourselves and did some experamints. And then we did this book to explain all this stuff and make lots of money. Huh-huh!

Yeah, heh-heh-heh! And all these scientific dudes are gonna buy this book and go, "Ohhh, yeah. I see now. I guess I was just a dumb-ass!" Heh-heh-heh-heh-heh!

And, uhh, some of our book is about science friction. Like, a lot of stuff about the unknown has to do with outer space and the future and stuff. And there's a lot of sci-fi movies and TV shows that are about that kind of crap too, so we thought we'd check some of them out. Maybe some of this sci-fi stuff'll help you understand the unknown better, in case you're, like, slow or something. Like those scientific dudes. Huh-huh-huh!

Heh-heh-heh! Yeah! Stupid buttholes! Heh-heh!

So, like, here we go. Just turn off the lights, get some nachos, sit back, relax, and uh, take off your pants (espeshully if you're a chick). Huh-huh-huh!

LIFE AFTER DEATH

EVERYONE'S ALWAYS LIKE, "UMM, IS THERE LIFE AFTER DEATH?" IT'S LIKE THIS BIG MYSTERY AND NOBODY KNOWS THE ANSWER. SO, LIKE, ME AND BUTT-HEAD WANTED TO DO AN EXPEARMINT TO FIND OUT THE TRUTH. WE FOUND THIS COOL DEAD THING IN THE ROAD. HEH-HEH! I THINK IT WAS A GOAT. THEN WE WATCHED IT TO SEE IF THERE WAS LIFE AFTER DEATH. I TOOK A BUNCH OF NOTES AND STUFF. CHECK IT OUT.

DAY 1: WE WATCHED THIS DEAD GOAT. HEH-HEH ALL DAY. HEH-HEH. IT WAS PRETTY COOL 'CUZ IT WAS ALL SMASHED AND YOU COULD SEE ITS GUTS AND STUFF. IT WAS DEAD. HEH-HEH-UMM-HEH-HEH.

DAY 2: UMM, THE GOAT STILL DIDN'T MOVE OR ANYTHING. BUT IT WAS STILL COOL, 'CUZ WE GOT TO SEE A LOT OF FLIES AND ANTS CRAWLING ON IT, HEH-HEH-HEH. I STEPPED ON SOME, HEH-HEH-HEH.

DAY 3: UMM, THIS DEAD THING IS STARTING TO SMELL. THAT'S COOL! BUTT-HEAD POKED IT WITH A STICK AND SOME JUNK LEAKED OUT OF ITS BUTT! HEH-HEH-HEH!

DAY 4: HEH-HEH-HEH. TRUCKS KEEP RUNNING OVER THE GOAT, AND NOW IT'S ALL FLAT AND KIND OF LOOKS LIKE THE HAIR AND STUFF IN MY BATH-TUB. HEH-HEH-HEH! I SPIT ON IT, BUT, UMM, IT STILL DIDN'T MOVE!

DAY 5: UMM, THIS EXPEARMINT SUCKS! IT'S, LIKE, WE KEEP WATCHING AND WATCHING, AND NOTHING HAPPENS! NYAAAAHHHHH! MOVE, DAMMIT! I'M GONNA KICK YOUR ASS, YOU SON OF A BITCH!

CONCLOOSHUN: WE DON'T KNOW WHY PEOPLE THINK LIFE AFTER DEATH IS SUCH A MYSTERY. THERE IS NO LIFE AFTER DEATH! AFTER DEATH, YOU JUST LAY THERE AND STINK AND GET ALL ROTTEN AND CROWS EAT YOUR EYES AND GUTS OUT. HEH-HEH!

MAGGOT-ALIENS FROM MARS

Umm, this is a picture of aliens from Mars! Some scientific dude on TV said that these maggots came from some rock that fell from Mars. Heh-heh! It was all over the news and stuff. It freaked us out cuz me and Butt-Head see these things all the time, but we never knew they were aliens!

So me and Butt-Head decided to find some of these maggot-aliens and kill them to protect Earth's women and stuff. Heh-heh! We knew where they hung out. It's like, their secret alien hide-out or something.

Yeah, huh-huh. We tipped over Anderson's garbage can and found a bunch of these maggot-aliens in there, crawling around on some old meat, huh-huh-huh. They were like all together and I think they were planning on how to take over the world and stuff. We took the leader of the maggot-aliens hostage and we tied it up and asked it a bunch of questions. We asked it what they were gonna do with Earth and when the invasion was gonna start. But it just kept quiet, so Beavis stomped on it and squished it. Huh-huh-huh. So then we went back and screamed at the maggot-aliens to surrender. But, like, they ignored us, so we stomped on all of them too. Huh-huh-huh!

Yeah, heh-heh! Umm, the women of Earth are safe now. So as an award, they should come do it with us! Heh-heh! That would rule!

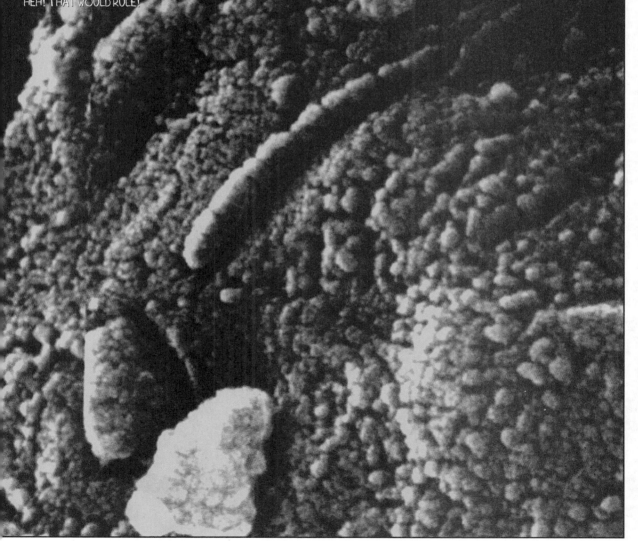

VOODOO DOLLS

So, like, Voodoo Dolls are cool. When you have a Voodoo Doll of someone, you have, like, total power over them. Cuz when you do something to a Voodoo Doll, it, like, really happens in real life. Like, if I took a Voodoo Doll of McVicker and threw it off a cliff, McVicker would really fall off a cliff, huh-huh-huh.

Yeah! Heh-heh! And, like, if I had a Voodoo Doll of Pamela Anderson and took off its clothes, then she'd be naked in real life! Heh-heh-heh!

Cool! Huh-huh. So, uhh, the way you make a Voodoo Doll is you take a doll from a little chick or an action figure from Beavis (huh-huh, he still plays with them). Then you take pieces of body stuff from the person you wanna do Voodoo to. Like, I was making a Voodoo Doll of Beavis. So I ripped a chunk of his hair out of his head. Then I taped it to a doll. Then when your doll's ready, you raise your arms and go, "Uggah-bugga-bluh-bluh-butt!"

Now the doll was all full of magic voodoo power and I had control over Beavis. Huh-huh! I started stabbing the doll in the head and that got Beavis pissed, so he tried to grab the doll. But he tripped and fell down and bashed his head on the edge of a table. So voodoo kicks ass.

STUFF TO DO WITH A VOODOO DOLL
OF SOMEONE THAT SUCKS

* Throw it at a wall, over and over.
* Stab it in the face with a nail.
* Hit it with a hammer.
* Stick it in your butt.
* Melt its weiner.
* Poop on it.
* Flush it down the toilet.
* Throw it up on someone's roof.
* Let a dog rip its head off.
* Put it on a bus that's going to another town.

PHONE PSYKICKS

PHONE PSYKICKS ARE THESE PEOPLE WHO, LIKE, ARE SUPPOSED TO KNOW WHAT'S GONNA HAPPEN AFTER IT HAPPENS, OR, UHH, SOMETHING. WE CALLED A PHONE PSYKICK TO SEE IF THEY'RE FOR REAL. HUH-HUH. THIS WAS LIKE, OUR CONVERSASHUN:

Welcome to the Psychic Pals Network.

HEY, BABY. UH-HUH-HUH.

Hi, would you like me to predict your future?

NO, HUH-HUH. BUT, UHH, DO YOU HAVE BIG BOOBS? HUH-HUH-HUH!

Excuse me? This is a psychic hotline, not a sex line.

UHH, OKAY. HUH-HUH. CAN YOU, UHH, PREDICT IF YOU'VE GOT BIG BOOBS? HUH-HUH-HUH-HUH!

I don't understand.

YEAH, HEH-HEH-HEH! CAN YOU, UMM, PREDICT IF YOU'RE NAKED? HEH-HEH-HEH-HEH! HUH-HUH! HUH-HUH-HUH! HEH-HEH-HEH-HEH! CAN YOU PREDICT IF I HAVE A STIFFY? HEH-HEH-HEH-HEH!

(CLICK)

CONCLOOSHUN: SHE WAS A REAL GOOD PHONE PSYKICK. AND SHE WAS PRETTY HOT. HUH-HUH. UHH, I CAN PREDICT STUFF TOO. I PREDICT STEWART'S GONNA GET HIS ASS KICKED WHEN HIS DAD GETS THE PHONE BILL. HUH-HUH-HUH!

DEMONIC POZESHUN

UHH, HUH-HUH. WHEN SOMEONE'S POZESSED BY THE DEVIL, YOU GOTTA, LIKE, DO THE SAME THINGS THAT THE PRIEST DUDE IN THAT ONE "EXORCIST" MOVIE DID:

UHH, HOW'S IT GOING, DEVIL? UHH, BE GONE OR SOMETHING, UH-HUH-HUH. UHH, OKAY, DEVIL DUDE, IF YOU'RE NOT GONNA LISTEN, I'M GONNA THROW HOLY WATER ON YOU. UH-HUH-HUH. BUT, LIKE, I DON'T GOT ANY, SO, UHH, I'LL THROW A FREEZY WHIP ON YOU, HUH-HUH-HUH.

UHH, OKAY, DEVIL. I'M GONNA PRAY. HUH-HUH. UHH, I PLEDGE A LEGION TO THE FLAG OF THE UNITED AMERICAS, OR SOMETHING. HMM. OKAY, THAT DIDN'T WORK. HOW ABOUT THIS. UHH, TAKE ME! HUH-HUH-HUH! TAKE ME INSTEAD AND STUFF! HUH-HUH-HUH. THAT WOULD BE COOL!

WHOA! HUH-HUH. SOMETHING'S HAPPENING.

I AM THE GREAT CORNHOLIO! I NEED T.P. FOR MY BUNGHOLE!

YOU DORK, YOU WEREN'T SUP-POSED TO DRINK THE FRUITY WHIP! NOW GET OUT OF BED, YOU LAZY DILL-WAD!

ARE YOU THREATENING ME?! YOU MUST BOW DOWN TO THE ALMIGHTY BUNGHOLE!

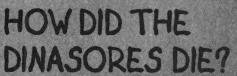

HOW DID THE DINASORES DIE?

UMM, THESE STUPID SCIENTISTS THINK THAT SOME BIG ROCK FROM OUTER-SPACE CRASHED INTO THE EARTH AND THAT'S WHY ALL THE DINASORES DIED. BUT THAT'S STUPID. HOW COULD ONE ROCK KILL ALL 100 DINASORES? THIS IS THE WAY IT REALLY HAPPENED.

LIKE, ONCE UPON A TIME, ALL DINASORES LIVED IN JAPAN. IT WAS PRETTY COOL 'CUZ, LIKE, THESE DINASORES WOULD EAT THE JAPAN PEOPLE AND KICK OVER THEIR BUILDINGS AND EAT THE BUILDINGS TOO, HEH-HEH-HEH. AND THEY'D BREATHE RADIASHUN AND FRY EVERYONE! YEAHHHH! OOOO-AHHHH! HEH-HEH-HMM-HEH-HEH! AND JAPANESE DUDES WOULD BE RUNNING AROUND SCREAMING! AND SOMETIMES THE DINASORES WOULD FIGHT EACH OTHER AND RIP EACH OTHER'S ARMS OUT AND SPLASH BLUE BLOOD ALL OVER THE PLACE AND THROW EACH OTHER AROUND THESE JAPAN CITIES AND WRECK EVERYTHING! HEH-HEH-HEH!

SO FINALLY THE JAPAN ARMY DUDES GOT ALL PISSED, HEH-HEH, AND THEY SENT OUT TANKS AND JETS AND STUFF. HEH-HEH-HEH! THEY SHOT BOMBS INTO THE DINOSORE'S HEADS AND KICKED THEIR ASSES! HEH-HEH-HEH! AND THEN THE DINASORES STARTED SPEWING BLUE BLOOD OUT OF THEIR GUTS AND SCREAMING AND MOST OF THEM DIED.

A FEW DINASORES DIDN'T WANNA GET KILLED, SO THEY GAVE UP. THEN THE JAPAN DUDES ROUNDED THEM UP AND SHOVED THEM IN MUSEUMS AND LOCKED EM IN. THE DINASORES, LIKE, LIVED THERE FOR AWHILE BUT THEY GOT TIRED OF WALKING AROUND THE MUSEUM LOOKING AT STUPID THINGS, SO THEY FELL DOWN AND DIED OF BOREDOM. AND YOU CAN STILL SEE THEIR BONES THERE. THAT'S COOL.

JURASSICK PARK

THIS MOVIE WAS PRETTY COOL, BUT, LIKE, IF ME AND BEAVIS DIRECTED IT, IT'D BE MUCH BETTER. CHECK IT OUT, HUH-HUH-HUH.

TAROT CARDS

HEH-HEH, WE FOUND SOME OF THESE, UMM, TAROT CARDS IN VAN DRIESSEN'S GARAGE, HEH-HEH. PEOPLE CAN USE THESE TO, YOU KNOW, TELL YOUR FUTURE OR SOMETHING IF YOU JUST PULL OUT SOME CARDS. HEH-HEH-HEH! "PULL OUT." UMM, THESE ARE THE ONES I PULLED AND LIKE, BUTT-HEAD TOLD ME MY FUTURE. IT WAS AMAZING! HE KNEW ALL THIS JUST BY LOOKING AT THESE CARDS:

(1) UHH, OKAY, BEAVIS. THIS CARD MEANS THAT IN THE FUTURE, A DUDE WEARING A BATH ROBE AND A MASK IS GONNA JUMP OUT AT YOU. THEN HE'S GONNA TAKE OFF HIS MASK AND HE'S GONNA BE A COOL SKULL DUDE UNDERNEATH. THEN HE'S GONNA TAKE THIS BIG KNIFE THAT'S ON A STICK AND HE'S GONNA CHOP YOU IN HALF AND WATCH YOU SQUIRM AROUND AND DIE. HUH-HUH-HUH!

(2) THIS CARD MEANS THAT IN THE FUTURE, YOU'RE GONNA SEE SOME FUNNY-LOOKING CHICK WITH A BUNCH OF ARMS WALKING DOWN THE STREET AND SHE'S GONNA BE TOP-LESS AND FEELING HER OWN BOOBS. HUH-HUH! THAT'S A COOL FUTURE!

(3) UHH, THIS CARD MEANS THAT IN THE FUTURE SOME UGLY HUNCHED-UP DUDE IS GONNA RUN BY YOU WAVING AROUND A BUNCH OF TOILET PAPER OR SOMETHING. UHH, I GUESS THAT'S A PRETTY COOL FUTURE, TOO.

CONCLOOSHUN: HEH-HEH! TAROT CARDS ARE AMAZING! MY FUTURE RULES! IT'S, LIKE, I CAN HARDLY WAIT OR SOMETHING! UMM, EXCEPT FOR THAT SKULL DUDE. HEH-HEH. WHEN I SEE HIM, I THINK I'M JUST GONNA TELL HIM THAT BUTT-HEAD'S REALLY THE ONE WHO PULLED THAT CARD!

AINCHENT EGYPT: THE SPHINXTER & THE GREAT PEERAMIDS

IN EGYPT, THERE'S A BUNCH OF MYSTERIOUS STUFF. BUT EVERYONE'S LIKE, REALLY CONFUSED ABOUT THESE THINGS CALLED THE GREAT PEERAMIDS AND THE SPHINXTER. HUH-HUH. IT'S, LIKE A BIG MYSTERY ABOUT WHAT THE HELL THEY ARE AND WHY THEY'RE THERE. SO, UHH, WE CHECKED IT OUT FOR OURSELVES, AND WE SOLVED THE MYSTERY.

A LONG TIME AGO, THE SPHINXTER WAS, LIKE, THE GOD OF BUTTS, HUH-HUH-HUH. IT'S LIKE, IF YOU HAD A PROBLEM WITH YOUR BUTT, YOU'D GO PRAY TO THE SPHINXTER, HUH-HUH-HUH. YOU'D BE, LIKE, "UHH, ALMIGHTY SPHINXTER. HUH-HUH-HUH. MY BUTT'S GOT PROBLEMS. FIX IT, DUDE." AND THEN, LIKE, YOU'D HAVE TO GO AROUND BACK AND SMELL THE SPHINXTER'S BUTT AND YOU'D BE OKAY. HUH-HUH-HUH-HUH!

ALL THESE PEOPLE KEPT COMING TO THE SPHINXTER AND COMPLAINING ABOUT THEIR ITCHY BUTT-CRACKS. HUH-HUH. THE SPHINXTER GOT SICK AND TIRED OF HEARING ABOUT IT, SO HE COMMANDED THEM TO BUILD THESE THINGS CALLED THE GREAT PEERAMIDS. AND HE ORDERED THAT WHEN SOMEONE HAD A ITCHY BUTT-CRACK THEY HAD TO CLIMB UP TO THE TOP OF A GREAT PEERAMID TO WHERE IT GOT ALL POINTY, HUH-HUH, THEN CROUCH DOWN AND ITCH THEIR BUTT-CRACKS WITH THE POINTY PART. HUH-HUH-HUH!

BEAVIS SHOULD BUILD ONE OF THOSE GREAT PEERAMIDS CUZ HE KEEPS USING THE EDGE OF THE KITCHEN TABLE AND, LIKE, NOW IT SMELLS FUNNY.

MUMMIES & KING BUTTUNCOMMON

MUMMIES ARE, LIKE, THESE DEAD DUDES FROM, LIKE, 100 YEARS AGO, THAT LIVED IN THE GREAT PEERAMIDS AND LIKED TO WRAP THEMSELVES UP IN TOILET PAPER AND HAD THEIR BRAINS PULLED OUT THROUGH THEIR NOSES, HEH-HEH-HEH. THEY WERE COOL.

SO, UHH, THE GREATEST MUMMY WHO EVER LIVED WAS THIS DUDE NAMED KING BUTTUNCOMMON, HUH-HUH-HUH. HE WAS PRETTY COOL LOOKING. UHH, SCIENTIFIC DUDES FOUND OUT STUFF ABOUT HIM FROM THESE DRAWINGS THEY FOUND ON A WALL. I THINK THEY CALL IT, UHH, HYDROGLIBICS OR SOMETHING. WE FOUND THIS IN SOME SCIENCE BOOK:

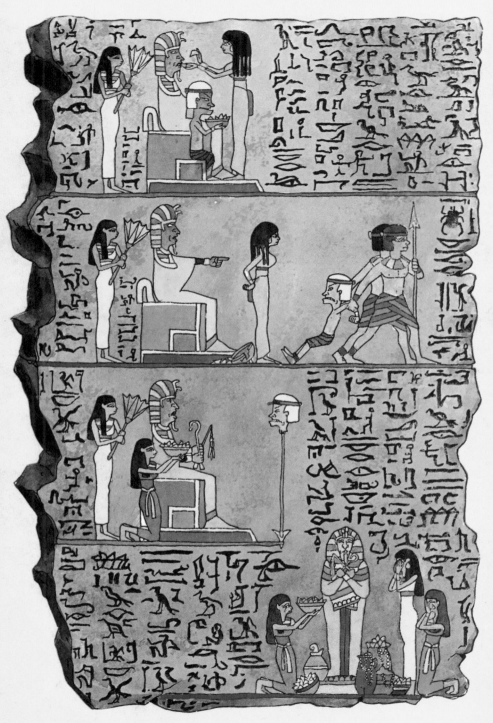

A strict and much-feared ruler, King Buttuncommon (1284-1269 B.C) had already reached the peak of his power and glory by age 14. As a result of a self-imposed law, King Butt was the only male in the kingdom allowed to have sexual relations. Thus, he enjoyed constant female attention. Besides women, King Butt always kept one loyal male slave, called a "Dum-as" at his side.

Any mistakes on the part of the slave were met with swift and terrible punishment, as shown here after the "Dum-as" had apparently dropped a bowl of the royal food. A replacement "Dum-as" would be found immediately.

King Butt died of what can only be called excessive intercourse. A study of his well-preserved remains revealed unusual wear on his genitalia. Thousands of women, now doomed by law to a life without sexual intercourse, mourned his death. King Butt was buried with items the Egyptians believed would serve him in the afterlife: gold, jewels, and several urns of flattened, baked-corn wedges mixed with a cheese-like substance.

THE ABDOMINAL SNOWMAN

HEY BUTTHEAD, ISN'T THIS, LIKE, THAT GIANT HAIRY THING THAT LIVES IN SOME MOUNTAINS?

UHH, I'VE GOT A GIANT HAIRY THING THAT LIVES IN MY PANTS, HUH-HUH-HUH-HUH.

OH, YEAH. HEH-HEH-HEH-HEH! ME TOO.

THIS THING IS CALLED THE, UHHH, ABDOMINAL SNOWMAN 'CUZ IT'S STOMACH IS ALL BUFF AND HARD, HUH-HUH-HUH. KINDA LIKE MINE. HE'S ALWAYS, YOU KNOW, WORKING OUT, GOIN' TO THE GYM AND STUFF.

THEN HE GOES TO THE MALL TO THAT ONE HEALTH STORE AND HE GETS THAT POWDER THAT'S SUPPOSED TO MAKE YOU ALL MUSCULAR.

YEAH-YEAH! HEH-HEH. I TRIED THAT STUFF! REMEMBER, BUTTHEAD? IT DIDN'T WORK TOO GOOD.

YEAH, YOU OPENED IT IN THE STORE AND ATE, LIKE, HALF THE CAN. HUH-HUH. THEN YOU STARTED CHOKING AND PUKING, HUH-HUH-HUH.

SHUT-UP, BUTTHEAD!

UH-HUH-HUH-HUH-HUH. SO, LIKE, HARDLY ANYBODY'S SEEN THE ABDOMINAL SNOWMAN, BUT, LIKE, IF YOU'RE A CHICK AND YOU SEE HIM, YOU GET ALL HORNY, HUH-HUH-HUH, AND, LIKE, YOU GOTTA, YOU KNOW, HAVE IT, HUH-HUH-HUH-HUH.

PSYKICK INVESTGATORS

There's these people who stand where something, you know, happened. Then they get these, uhhh, pictures in their heads about what was going on in that spot...huh-huh-huh-huh..."spot." I think they call it, uhh, "psykick flashes." This is like what happens to that dude on that "Millennium" show.

So, me and Butt-Head watched that show a bunch of times. And it sucked. Heh-heh. But, umm, we learned how to do those "psykick flashes."

Yeah. Huh-huh. It was cool. We, like, walked all over town and this is what we, you know, saw in our heads. It's, like, a gift or something. So, uhh, we decided to use it for mankind and stuff. Huh-huh-huh.

GIRL'S LOCKER-ROOM: Huh-huh-huh! We, like snuck in, closed our eyes and saw all these naked chicks everywhere! Huh-huh-huh! This rules!

Yeah! Yeah! Check it out! Bare chick ass! Heh-heh-heh-heh! Boobs everywhere! Look! Ahhhhh! Wet hooters!

SIDEWALK: We found a spot where we sensed that once a dog was taking a dump, heh-heh-heh! I, like, saw it real clear in my mind and stuff. Heh-heh! Even though I was kinda distracted and stuff cuz I was standing in a turd and it stunk.

THE COOLER AT BURGER WORLD: Umm, heh-heh, this was where I sensed some dude was once just standing around with his shlong hanging out of his pants, heh-heh-heh. Umm, ohhh yeah. Heh-heh-hmm-heh-heh. That was me.

THE ALLEY: We went in this dark alley and there was all these cops running around and there was a drawing of a dude on the ground. There was all this yellow tape all over the place and a burned-up car that was full of little holes. We, like, stood there and closed our eyes and we sensed that one time, a garbageman was there and he hocked a big loogie! Heh-heh-heh! That ruled!

BEAVIS' KITCHEN: This was where we sensed some guy with a moustache scoring with Beavis' mom, huh-huh-huh-huh. Oh, yeah. And some dude with a pony-tail. And a fat guy with a bunch of tattoos, huh-huh-huh. Some Mexican guy, then a tall dude with a cowboy hat, and a couple of cops. Huh-huh! Huh-huh-huh-huh!

Heh-heh-heh. She's a slut.

Yeah. Huh-huh. It was probably all in one night. Huh-huh-huh!

WITCHCRAFT

UHH, THIS IS, LIKE, THE ONLY KNOWN PICTURE OF WITCHES...IN THE WORLD AND STUFF. HUH-HUH. JUST THE CHICKS, THOUGH. THAT DUDE ISN'T A WITCH, HUH-HUH-HUH. HE'S JUST A DORK.

HEY, BUTT-HEAD, ISN'T THIS THAT SHOW THAT'S ON, UMM, NICKIMMODIUM?

SHUT-UP, BEAVIS! IT'S, LIKE, YOU HAVE TO RUIN EVERYTHING! BUNGHOLE! HUH-HUH. SO, ANYWAY, LIKE THIS WITCH DOES SOMETHING WITH HER NOSE....UHH, I THINK SHE PICKS IT, HUH-HUH, AND THEN MAGIC CRAP HAPPENS.

BUT, LIKE, IF YOU'RE A WITCH AND THE COPS CATCH YOU, THEY, UMM, BURN YOUR STEAK.

UHH, WHAT?

IT'S PROBABLY, LIKE, ONE OF THE COPS HOLDS YOU DOWN AND THE OTHERS MESS UP YOUR KITCHEN AND THE FRIDGE LOOKING FOR SOME STEAK, THEN THEY FRY IT UP UNTIL IT'S ALL BLACK AND BURNED, SO NO ONE CAN EAT IT. HEH-HEH-HEH. IT'S LIKE, REALLY MEAN.

NO, DUMBASS. HUH-HUH. I THINK THE ONLY WAY YOU KILL A WITCH IS TO THROW WATER ON HER. THEN SHE LIKE, MELTS AND TURNS INTO A BUNCH OF PUKE AND STUFF. HUH-HUH-HUH.

YEAH! YEAH! HEY, BUTT-HEAD, IF A WITCH WAS CHASING ME, I'D, LIKE, STOP AT THE WATER FOUNTAIN AND DRINK SOME WATER REAL FAST, HEH-HEH. THEN I'D TURN AROUND AND SPIT IT ON HER, HEH-HEH-HEH. SHE'D BE, LIKE, "AGGGHHH!" AND I'D JUST BE STANDING THERE, GOING "YOU'RE LUCKY I DIDN'T BURN YOUR STEAK, BEE-OTCH!"

UHH, SOME WITCHES DO THESE THINGS CALLED MAGIC SPELLS, WHERE THEY MIX UP SOME STUFF IN A BIG POT AND SAY SOME MAGIC WORDS OR SOMETHING AND THEN STUFF THEY WANT TO HAPPEN COMES TRUE! ME AND BEAVIS THOUGHT THAT WAS A PRETTY COOL IDEA, SO WE MADE SOME MAGIC SPELLS, TOO. I GUESS YOU CAN USE THEM IF YOU WANT.

MAGIC SPELL FOR GETTING MONEY

FIRST, YOU GET A BIG POT OR SOMETHING. THEN YOU GET THIS STUFF AND, LIKE, THROW IT IN THE POT:

WINGS OF FLY.
EARS OF MOTH.
MUD.
BUTT OF CENTIPEED.
TURD OF DOG.
WEINER OF GRASSHOPPER.
LEFTOVER RAT GUTS FROM BIOLOGY CLASS.

THEN YOU, LIKE, MIX IT ALL UP AND THROW IT AT STEWART'S WINDOW UNTIL HE COMES OUT. HUH-HUH-HUH. SO THEN, LIKE, WHEN HE COMES OUT YOU HAVE TO, UHH, SAY THESE MAGIC WORDS OR SOMETHING: "STEWART, I'LL, LIKE, LET YOU HANG OUT WITH ME IF YOU GIMME FIVE BUCKS." HUH-HUH-HUH. IT'S A PRETTY COOL SPELL 'CUZ IT ALWAYS WORKS.

Magic Spell For Being Cool

For this spell to work, you need money. So, umm, do the "Magic Spell To Get Money" first. Then, you need to mix-up these magic ingredients:

Puke of cat.
Leftover frog guts from biology class.
Dead squirrel.
A fish brain.
Turd of Beavis.

Umm, heh-heh, then you take all this and leave it in Anderson's mailbox, heh-heh-heh! After that you, like, find Todd. First you tell him what you did to Anderson, heh-heh. Then you say these magic words: "Umm, hey man, can I be in your gang? Heh-heh, I got money." Then he'll say something like "Gimme that money or I'll rip your head off." When you give Todd the money he'll, like, drive away. But you'll be pretty cool now, heh-heh, see, 'cuz Todd talked to you and he didn't kick your ass.

A Magic Spell To Get Food

Mix-up these magic things:

1 dead, rotten bird
Stomped-on worm guts
12 cockroaches.
Head of cricket.
Turd of cat.

So then, like, put all this stuff in your hands and, umm, take it to the food cort at the mall, heh-heh. Then walk up to some chicks that are eating and, like, show it to them. Heh-heh-heh-heh! Lots of times, they'll scream and run away. Heh-heh-heh. Then you can sit down and eat their food! If you go wash your hands, the chicks might change their minds and come back for their food, so better wait 'til you're done eating.

Magic Spell For Beavis To Score

This is, like, a spell that only works on Beavis. If Beavis messes up, huh-huh-huh, he won't score. First, he has to, like, eat all these things:

A handful of worms.
Some dirt.
Junk from the grease trap at Burger World
A stick.
Buzzcut's jock-strap.

After Beavis, like, eats all this stuff, huh-huh-huh, tell him he can't watch TV or spank his monkey or eat nachos or take a dump for a week. Huh-huh-huh-huh! Only then will he score.

Huh-huh-huh! This spell rules cuz it's cool to watch Beavis try and eat all that stuff.

STONE HENDGE

WHOA! UMM, ISN'T THIS THAT THING? THE EYEFULL TOWER?

UHH, NO, DUMBASS. THE EYEFULL TOWER IS THAT THING IN FRANCE THAT'S JUST, LIKE, A BUNCH OF GIRDERS AND CRAP. AND LIKE, NOBODY IN FRANCE WANTS TO FINISH BUILDING IT BECAUSE THEY'RE A BUNCH OF LAZY, WHINING BUTT-HOLES, HUH-HUH-HUH-HUH!

OH, YEAH, HEH-HEH-HEH-HEH!

THESE ARE JUST A BUNCH OF BIG ROCKS IN NEW ENGLAND THAT SOME AINCHENT DUDES PUT UP. IT'S SUPPOSED TO BE AN OLD CALENDER OR SOMETHING. HUH-HUH. BUT THIS CALENDER SUCKS AND THE AINCHENT DUDES THAT MADE IT MUST'VE BEEN STUPID OR SOMETHING.

IT'S LIKE, THE AINCHENT DUDES WOULD GET UP EVERY MORNING AND GET SOME COFFEE AND BRUSH THEIR TEETH AND GO LOOK AT THIS STONE HENDGE CALENDER TO SEE WHAT DAY IT WAS AND THEY'D JUST STARE AT THE ROCKS AND BE LIKE, "UHH, THERE'S NO NUMBERS OR DAYS OR ANYTHING! IT'S JUST A DAMN BUNCH OF ROCKS! THIS SUCKS! I DON'T KNOW IF IT'S SATURDAY OR IF I GOTTA GO TO WORK! DAMMIT! I HATE THIS STUPID CALENDER!"

YEAH, REALLY! IT'S, LIKE, IF IT WAS A NORMAL CALENDER, IT'D HAVE NUMBERS ON IT AND PICTURES OF BARE-ASS CHICKS LAYING ALL OVER CARS! HEH-HEH!

MENTAL TELEPATHY

UHH, HUH-HUH, ME AND BEAVIS SAW SOME DUDE ON TV READING PEOPLE'S MINDS. SO, LIKE, I READ SOME PEOPLE'S MINDS TOO. AND THIS IS WHAT THEY WERE, UHH, THINKING:

ANDERSON: "I'M OLD. AND I SUCK."

STEWART: "I LIKE WINGER AND I SUCK MORE THAN ANYONE HAS SUCKED BEFORE."

VAN DRIESSEN: "I'M A WUSSY. SOMEONE SHOULD KICK MY ASS."

STEWART'S MOM: "BUTT-HEAD RULES. I WANT HIM. OH YEAH, AND STEWART SUCKS!"

BUZZCUT: "STEWART AND VAN DRIESSEN SUCK. I SHOULD KICK THEIR ASS. I SUCK, TOO. I SHOULD KICK MY OWN ASS."

BEAVIS: "HEY, HOW'S IT GOIN'?"

BUTT-HEAD: "I'M THE COOLEST DUDE EVER. I CAN EVEN, LIKE, READ MY OWN MIND. THIS IS COOL."

THE X-FILES

THE X-FILES TEACHES YOU ALL ABOUT UNKNOWN STUFF, SO THAT'S COOL. BUT THE SHOW JUST SUCKS CUZ IT'S ALL CONFUSING AND IT ACTUALLY TRIES TO MAKE YOU THINK. THIS IS HOW WE WOULD DO IT:

U.F.O. SIGHTINGS

U.F.O STANDS FOR, UHH, UNDER-IDENTIFIED FLYING CRAP. THERE'S ALL THESE PEOPLE WHO SAY THEY SAW U.F.O'S, AND THERE'S EVEN, LIKE, PICTURES OF THESE THINGS. CHECK "EM OUT.

THESE PICTURES SUCK, HEH-HEH-HEH. THEY'RE, LIKE, FAKE! HEH-HEH-HEH.

YEAH, REALLY. WHAT A DAMN RIP-OFF! SO, LIKE, WE TOOK SOME REAL PICTURES OF U.F.O'S. HUH-HUH-HUH. CHECK THIS OUT.

UMM, ME AND BUTT-HEAD TOOK THIS PICTURE. HEH-HEH. OUT OF A MAGAZINE, HEH-HEH. I WAS, LIKE, WHOA! WHAT THE HELL IS THAT THING! I'M, LIKE, PRETTY SURE THIS A U.F.O OR SOMETHING.

UHHH, IT KINDA LOOKS LIKE A DOG, BUT IT'S, LIKE, DOGS DON'T FLY. HUH-HUH.

YEAH! YEAH! SEE WHAT I MEAN? HEH-HEH. THIS PICTURE SCARED THE CRAP OUT OF ME!

UHH, ME AND BEAVIS TOOK THIS PICTURE IN THE PARK. THIS U.F.O THING WAS, LIKE, FLOATING AROUND UP IN THE AIR AND STUFF.

YEAH, HEH-HEH, IT WAS CHASING DOWN SOME DUDE. HE WAS TRYING TO RUN AWAY FROM IT BUT, LIKE, IT KEPT FOLLOWING HIM WHEREVER HE WENT. HEH-HEH-HEH. ME AND BUTTHEAD GOT AWAY, BUT THAT GUY PROBABLY GOT KILLED WITH A DEATH RAY OR SOME-THING. HEH-HEH-HEH.

UHH, THIS IS A REAL QUIET U.F.O. SO IT CAN SNEAK UP ON YOU. WHEN IT WENT BY, WE SAW IT HAD A HUMAN PRIS-ONER. HE WAS WAVING AT US, PROBA-BLY FOR US TO SAVE HIM. BUT, LIKE, WHEN ME AND BEAVIS CHUCKED SOME ROCKS AT THE U.F.O, THE PRISONER GUY STARTED SWEARING AT US. WHATEVER, DUDE. HUH-HUH. SOME PEOPLE JUST DON'T APPRECIATE HELP.

HOW TO FAKE A U.F.O. SIGHTING

UMM, SOME DUDES TAKE, LIKE, FAKE PICTURES OF UFO'S AND, LIKE, SELL IT TO THE GOVERMINT AND NEWSPAPERS AND STUFF! HEH-HEH-HEH! IF YOU WANNA, LIKE, MAKE MONEY, HERE'S HOW TO, UMM, TAKE FAKE UFO PICTURES AND STUFF. YOU NEED A CAMERA AND, LIKE, A GARBAGE CAN LID OR SOMETHING. HEH-HEH-HEH.

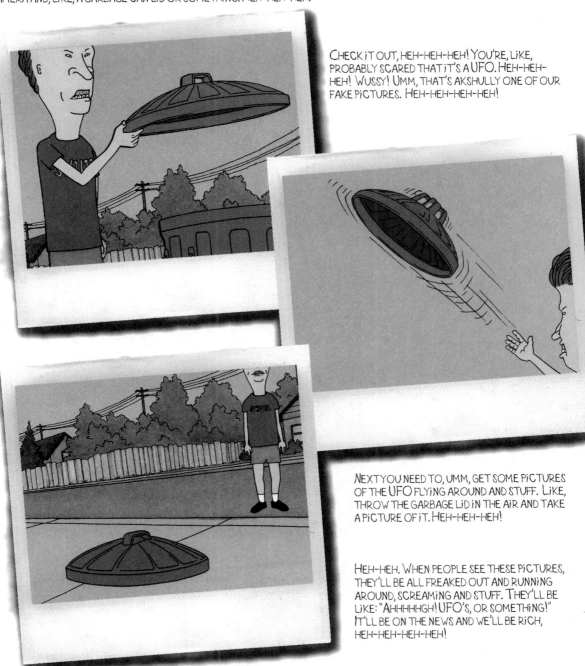

CHECK IT OUT, HEH-HEH-HEH! YOU'RE, LIKE, PROBABLY SCARED THAT IT'S A UFO. HEH-HEH-HEH! WUSSY! UMM, THAT'S AKSHULLY ONE OF OUR FAKE PICTURES. HEH-HEH-HEH-HEH!

NEXT YOU NEED TO, UMM, GET SOME PICTURES OF THE UFO FLYING AROUND AND STUFF. LIKE, THROW THE GARBAGE LID IN THE AIR AND TAKE A PICTURE OF IT. HEH-HEH-HEH!

HEH-HEH. WHEN PEOPLE SEE THESE PICTURES, THEY'LL BE ALL FREAKED OUT AND RUNNING AROUND, SCREAMING AND STUFF. THEY'LL BE LIKE: "AHHHHHGH! UFO'S, OR SOMETHING!" IT'LL BE ON THE NEWS AND WE'LL BE RICH, HEH-HEH-HEH-HEH!

INDEPENDUNCE DAY

HUH-HUH! THE FIRST PART OF THIS MOVIE RULED!

YEAH! YEAH! HEH-HEH! EVERYTHING JUST BLEW UP! YAHHHHHH! HOOOOWAHHH! HEH-HEH-HEH-HEH-HEH!

UMM, IT'S, LIKE, I USED TO THINK ABOUT CHICKS WHEN I SPANK MY MONKEY. HEH-HEH-HEH. BUT NOW WHEN I DO IT, UMM, I THINK ABOUT THAT PART OF THE MOVIE, HEH-HEH-HEH-HEH-HEH!

BUT THEN, LIKE, THE REST OF THE MOVIE SUCKED. HUH-HUH-HUH. THERE WAS, LIKE, NO ALIENS. IT WAS JUST A BUNCH OF DORKS GOING "BLAH-BLAH-BLAH-BLAH!" SO, UHH, I THINK THE POINT WAS THAT WHEN ALIENS BLOW UP THE WORLD, THEY'RE ONLY GONNA LET BORING, STUPID ASS-MUNCHES LIVE. HUH-HUH-HUH. LIKE BEAVIS.

YEAH. YEAH, THAT'D BE NICE OF THEM. HEH-HEH. IF I DID THIS MOVIE, AND I HAD A GIANT SPACESHIP LIKE THAT, I'D LIKE BLOW UP OUR SCHOOL, HEH-HEH-HEH-HEH! THEN I'D BLOW UP BURGERWORLD! HEH-HEH! THEN I'D BLOW UP THE STUPID BUTTHOLES WHO MADE THIS PIECE OF CRAP MOVIE! HEH-HEH!

YEAH, HUH-HUH! THE ONLY GOOD THING ABOUT THIS MOVIE IS THAT THEY TOTALLY RIPPED-OFF EVERY SCI-FI MOVIE EVER MADE AND STUCK IT IN ONE MOVIE. SO, LIKE, NOW YOU DON'T HAVE TO RENT ALL THOSE SCI-FI MOVIES, YOU CAN JUST WATCH THIS ONE AND SAVE YOUR MONEY FOR SOMETHING COOL, LIKE PORN.

CURSES

IN THE OLD DAYS IF YOU PISSED SOMEONE OFF, THEY'D PUT A CURSE ON YOU. THEY'D BE, LIKE, "MAY ALL YOUR GUTS BLOW UP." AND SO YOUR GUTS WOULD JUST BLOW UP ALL OVER THE PLACE AND YOU'D JUST BE LAYING THERE, DEAD. HUH-HUH.

YEAH, HEH-HEH. WE FIGURED OUT WHY IT WORKED. IT'S CUZ IF YOU SAY THE WORD "MAY," YOU'RE BEING ALL POLITE TO THE POWERS OF DARKNESS OR SOME-THING. SO THE POWERS OF DARKNESS LIKE IT WHEN YOU KISS THEIR BUTT. HEH-HEH. THEN THEY DO WHAT YOU ASK TO THE PERSON YOU'RE PISSED AT.

ONE TIME I WAS, LIKE, "BUTT-HEAD, MAY YOU TURN INTO A BIG GIANT DOG TURD! HEH-HEH!"

YEAH. HUH-HUH. THEN I WAS LIKE, "BEAVIS, MAY YOU TURN INTO A STUPID LITTLE PRE-SCHOOL CHICK. HUH-HUH-HUH!"

SO, LIKE, THAT WORKED PRETTY GOOD AND STUFF. HUH-HUH. THEN I WAS, LIKE, "BEAVIS, MAY YOUR BUNGHOLE RIP UP IN, LIKE, A HUNDRED PIECES AND ALL THE REST OF YOUR SKIN, TOO! HUH-HUH-HUH!"

AND I WAS, LIKE, "BUTT-HEAD, MAY YOU SUCK MORE THAN ANY-BODY HAS EVER SUCKED BEFORE!" HEH-HEH-HMM-HEH! AND IT WORKED CUZ BUTT-HEAD TURNED INTO KENNY G!

EASTER ISLAND

Umm, Easter Island is the place where the Easter Bunny lives! Heh-heh! He, like, rules the island and all the people that live there are his slaves and have to bow down and worship him or he throws eggs at their house, heh-heh-heh!

But, like, the big mystery about Easter Island is these, umm, giant statues that are on the island. Umm, I figured it out. The Easter Bunny's slaves made these giant bunny statues out of chocolate to honor the Easter Bunny and stuff. One time, some dude got hungry and ate the ears off all the statues and then the Easter Bunny got pissed and shoved a egg up his butt. Heh-heh-heh! It was pretty cool!

All the scientific dudes all over the world don't understand how those giant statues got erected. Heh-heh-heh-heh-heh! Erected. Umm, I said it before and I'll say it again: Those scientific dudes are a bunch of stupid buttholes! Heh-heh. It's, like, the slaves took a giant crane and some bulldozers and they put up the statues. I mean, like, what's the big mystery? Heh-heh. If I ever see some of those scientific dudes, I'm gonna kick their asses!

GHOSTS

THERE WAS THIS SHOW ON TV WITH PEOPLE TALKING ABOUT GHOSTS AND SAYING HOW GHOSTS SLAPPED THEM AND SCREAMED AT THEM AND THREW EVERYTHING ALL OVER THEIR HOUSE. HEH-HEH! GHOSTS ARE COOL! BUT, UMM, THEY'RE STILL PRETTY FREAKY. HEH-HEH. UMM, HEY BUTT-HEAD. DO YOU, LIKE, BELIEVE IN GHOSTS?

UHH, YEAH, BUTT-GHOSTS, HUH-HUH-HUH-HUH!

OHHH YEAH, HEH-HEH. BUT, UMM, I MEAN REAL GHOSTS. CUZ, UMM, LIKE LAST NIGHT I HEARD THESE BIG FOOT-STEPS, AND SLAMMING DOORS, AND SOME GHOST DUDE LAUGHING.

WHOA! THAT'S PRETTY COOL, HUH-HUH-HUH.

YEAH, AND THEN A LITTLE LATER, HEH-HEH-HEH, THERE WAS THIS BANGING AND MOANING, AND I KEPT HEARING THIS CREAKY SOUND OVER AND OVER. IT WAS PRETTY SCARY, BUTT-HEAD.

UHH... HUH-HUH-HUH, YOU BUTT-MONKEY! THAT WAS YOUR MOM AND HER BOYFRIEND. HUH-HUH-HUH-HUH!

OHHH YEAH, HEH-HEH-HEH. SHE'S A SLUT.

GHOSTS ARE COOL 'CUZ THEY'RE LIKE, INDIVISIBLE OR SOMETHING. THEY CAN DO ANYTHING THEY WANT AND NOBODY SEES THEM. HERE'S SOME COOL STUFF WE'D DO IF WE WERE GHOSTS, HUH-HUH-HUH:

HEH-HEH-HEH-HEH-HEH-HEH. PLOP!

HEH-HEH-HEH, PEEK-A-BOO!

WHOA! HUH-HUH-HUH, THIS IS THE COOLEST THING EVER!

UHH, THIS IS, LIKE, THE BEST THING ABOUT BEING A GHOST.
YEAH! TV! HEH-HEH-HEH! TURN ON BAYWATCH!

OTHER STUFF THAT'S PRETTY COOL TO DO WHEN YOU'RE A INDIVISIBLE GHOST:

* LOOK AT PORN AT MAXI-MART.
* SPEND ALL NIGHT HANGING AROUND IN THE PARKING LOT AT MAXI-MART.
* WHEN YOU GO TO SCHOOL, YOU CAN SLEEP IN CLASS AND NOBODY'LL WAKE YOU UP, HUH-HUH-HUH.
* WHEN YOU GO TO THE MOVIES, CUT TO THE FRONT OF THE LINE AND BUY YOUR TICKETS BEFORE EVERYONE ELSE.
* HANG OUT AT THE MALL AND FOLLOW CHICKS AND THINK ABOUT WHAT THEY LOOK LIKE NAKED.

THE BERMUDA TRIANGLE

UHH, THE BERMUDA TRIANGLE, HUH-HUH-HUH, IS THIS PLACE IN, UHH, VIRGINIA, UH-HUH-HUH-HUH-HUH-HUH-HUH! AND IT'S, LIKE, THE COOLEST PLACE ON EARTH. HUH-HUH-HUH! STUDS LIKE ME ARE ALWAYS GOING THERE, HUH-HUH-HUH!

WHOA! REALLY?!

AND THERE'S ALWAYS THESE THINGS THAT GET LOST IN IT, HUH-HUH-HUH, LIKE ROCKETS AND SUBMARINES, HUH-HUH-HUH, AND TRAINS AND SNAKES, UH-HUH-HUH-HUH-HUH-HUH! HUH-HUH-HUH-HUH-HUH-HUH-HUH!

WHOA! THAT SOUNDS LIKE A PRETTY SCARY PLACE! LIKE, UMM, YOU CAN DIE! WHY THE HELL WOULD ANYONE GO THERE?

HUH-HUH-HUH! YOU DORK. THE BERMUDA TRIANGLE IS LIKE A BIG MYSTERY FOR BUTT-MUNCHES LIKE YOU, BEAVIS. YOU'LL PROBABLY NEVER SEE IT IN YOUR WHOLE LIFE, HUH-HUH-HUH-HUH!

WELL GOOD, DAMMIT! IT SOUNDS LIKE IT'D SUCK ANYWAYS! YOU CAN GO THERE. BUT NOT ME. NO, SIR. HEH-HEH. I'M JUST GONNA STAY RIGHT HERE AT HOME.

HUH-HUH-HUH! DUMBASS!

THE SHROUD OF TURIN

THE SHROUD OF TURIN IS THIS REALLY OLD PIECE OF CLOTH IN A MUSEUM SOMEWHERE. IT'S GOT THIS PICTURE OF SOME DUDE'S FACE ON IT. SOME GUY ON TV SAID IT'S LIKE, THAT ONE RELIGIOUS DUDE, JESUS, THAT DIED A LONG TIME AGO. THEY SAY THAT WHEN JESUS DIED HE GOT, LIKE, WRAPPED UP IN THIS OLD SHEET, AND AFTER A WHILE YOU COULD SEE HIS PICTURE ON IT. BUT, UHH, SOME OTHER PEOPLE THINK IT'S FAKE. HUH-HUH.

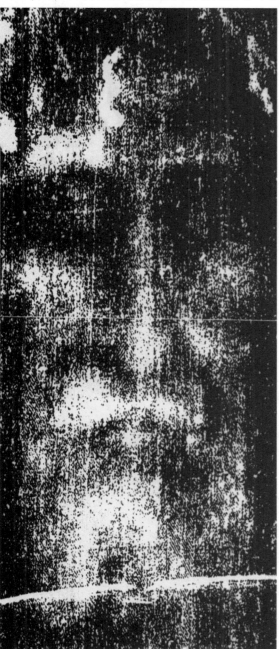

ME AND BEAVIS TRIED TO COPY WHAT HAPPENED TO THAT RELIGIOUS DUDE. WE WANTED TO SEE IF WE COULD MAKE A PICTURE OF BEAVIS ON A SHEET TOO, TO PROVE THAT THE SHROUD OF TURIN IS REAL. HUH-HUH. SO, UHH, I KICKED BEAVIS' ASS UNTIL HE LOOKED LIKE HE WAS DEAD AND STUFF.

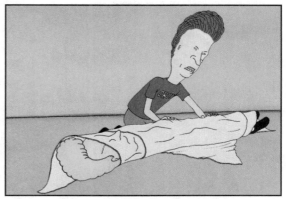

AFTER THAT, I ROLLED-UP BEAVIS IN A BEDSHEET.

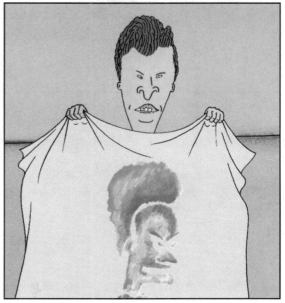

LIKE, A FEW DAYS LATER, I UNROLLED BEAVIS AND THERE WAS A PICTURE OF HIM ON THE SHEET! IT, LIKE, REALLY WORKED!

PSYKICK LINKS

PSYKICK LINKS IS WHEN, UHH, SOMETHING HAPPENS TO ONE PERSON AND SOME OTHER PERSON WHO'S, LIKE, SOMEWHERE FAR AWAY GETS THIS FEELING THAT SOMETHING HAPPENED TO THAT OTHER PERSON, OR SOMETHING.

UMM...WHAT?

UHH, I THINK THIS HAPPENED TO ME AND BEAVIS ONCE. I WAS AT HOME TAKING A DUMP AND BEAVIS WAS OUT RIDING HIS BIKE. ALL OF A SUDDEN I STARTED LAUGHING, FOR NO REASON. I WAS, LIKE, "I BET BEAVIS JUST WIPED OUT, HUH-HUH-HUH! WIPED."

WHOA! HEH-HEH-HEH!

SO, LIKE, A COUPLE MINUTES LATER BEAVIS SHOWED UP AND HE WAS ALL BLOODY AND LIMPING AND STUFF. HUH-HUH-HUH!

OHHH, YEAH. HEH-HEH! AND I HAD A PSYKICK LINK, TOO. CUZ WHEN I WIPED OUT, I WAS FALLING AND I WAS THINKING, "I BET BUTT-HEAD IS TAKING A DUMP, HEH-HEH-HEH!"

NOCTURNAL MISSIONS

There's this, like, beautiful miracle that happens to dudes, huh-huh-huh-huh, called "Nocturnal Missions", uh-huh-huh-huh-huh-huh! It's, like, huh-huh-huh, when you, like, huh-huh-huh-huh-huh-huh, wake-up and you just, uh-huh-huh-huh, inoculated. Huh-huh-huh-huh-huh-huh!

Heh-heh-heh-heh-heh-heh-heh! It's the most amazing thing ever! It's, like, you don't even have to spank your monkey! Hee-hee-heh-heh! And, heh-heh-heh, it happens anyway! Sometimes, heh-heh-heh, that happens when I fall asleep in class, heh-heh-heh-heh! You wake-up and you're, like, "Whoa!! Heh-heh!"

HUH-HUH, YEAH. THEN YOU'RE, LIKE, "UHH, EXCUSE ME, I GOTTA, LIKE, GO TO THE BATHROOM! HUH-HUH!"
OHHH, YEAH! HEH-HEH. THEN I HAFTA LIKE, FLUSH MY UNDERWEAR, HEH-HEH-HEH.
HUH-HUH-HUH-HUH! SO, UHH, ME AND BEAVIS THINK IT HAS TO DO WITH WHAT YOU'RE DREAMING ABOUT AND STUFF. WE DID A STUDY OR SOMETHING. CHECK IT OUT. HERE'S SOME OF THE DREAMS THAT CAUSED OUR, HUH-HUH-HUH, "NOCTURNAL MISSIONS."

LOCKNESS MONSTER

THERE'S THIS OTHER PLACE CALLED SCOTCHLAND OR SOMETHING, WHERE ALL THE DUDES ARE A BUNCH OF DRUNKS WHO WEAR DRESSES, HEH-HEH-HEH! WUSSIES! AND THEY MAKE MUSIC BY SQUEEZING THEIR BAGS, HEH-HEH-HEH! I'M GONNA TRY THAT—OWW! HEH-HEH-HEH! HEY, THAT KINDA SOUNDED LIKE BUSH, HEH-HEH-HEH!

SO, LIKE, IN SCOTCHLAND, THERE'S THIS POND WHERE THE LOCK NESS MONSTER LIVES. SOME PEOPLE SAY IT'S, LIKE, THIS DINO-SORE THAT NEVER DIED. BUT IT CAN'T BE, CUZ IF IT WAS, JAPAN WOULD'VE ATTACKED IT A LONG TIME AGO. PLUS IT WOULD'VE DROWNED.

NOBODY KNOWS WHAT IT IS OR WHAT IT LOOKS LIKE, CUZ ALL THE PICTURES SUCK. THE BIG MYSTERY IS WHY THESE DORKS IN SCOTCHLAND CAN'T TAKE A DECENT PICTURE. THE PICTURES ARE ALWAYS ALL BLURRY AND FAR AWAY, AND THE MONSTER JUST LOOKS LIKE A BUNCH OF GARBAGE FLOATING IN THE WATER. HEH-HEH! I THINK IT'S CUZ PEOPLE IN SCOTCHLAND ARE TOO DAMN DRUNK TO TAKE A GOOD PICTURE. HEH-HEH!

AND NO ONE IN SCOTCHLAND'LL EVER CATCH THE LOCK NESS MONSTER, CUZ THE DUDES ARE SUCH WUSSIES THAT THEY'RE AFRAID TO GET THEIR DRESSES WET. PLUS THEY'RE TOO BUSY SITTING AROUND SQUEEZING THEIR BAGS. HEH-HEH-HEH! IF THE LOCK NESS MONSTER WAS IN AMERICA, WE'D JUST DRAIN ALL THE WATER OUT OF THE POND AND PULL THE MONSTER OUT AND KICK ITS ASS. HEH-HEH-HEH! NONE OF THAT WUSSY CRAP!

IS ELVIS ALIVE?

Uhh, lots of years ago, there was this young, skinny dude that used to play Elvis. He was pretty cool. He played guitar and acted in movies about the beach and got lots of chicks. He even scored with Lisa Marie Presley. Huh-huh-huh.

Then something happened to the cool Elvis. I think he quit. Anyway, then this older, fat dude started playing Elvis. He sucked. He just ran around in a white cape, eating donuts and singing songs that still suck today.

The only reason the fat Elvis was famous is cuz he shot his TV with a gun. Huh-huh! Oh, yeah, and he was famous cuz he died on the toilet. He was trying to take a dump, huh-huh, and he pushed too hard and died. Huh-huh-huh!

Now there's like, all these TV shows and newspapers and stuff saying that it's, like, a big mystery if Elvis is really dead and stuff. So, uhh, me and Beavis dug up his grave to find out for sure. Huh-huh-huh.

Elvis' grave was cool! It smelled real bad, but there was, like, bones and old clothes and stuff. Beavis kept the skull. He put it on his toilet to remind him not to push too hard. Huh-huh-huh!

Conclooshun: Uhh...yeah, he's dead.

E.T.: THE EXTRA-TESTICLE

IT WAS COOL WHEN E.T. MADE THAT KID'S BIKE FLY AND STUFF. SO WE TRIED THAT. WE DROVE MY BIKE OFF BEAVIS' GARAGE. HUH-HUH. WE FLEW FOR, LIKE, A SECOND. THEN WE FELL AND BROKE A BUNCH OF BONES AND STUFF. HUH-HUH. "OUUUCH."

THIS MOVIE DIDN'T MAKE SENSE. IT'S, LIKE, E.T. COULD MAKE THINGS FLY. SO WHY DIDN'T HE JUST MAKE HIMSELF FLY UP INTO SPACE TO HIS OWN PLANET IF HE WANTED TO GO HOME SO DAMN MUCH. HUH-HUH.

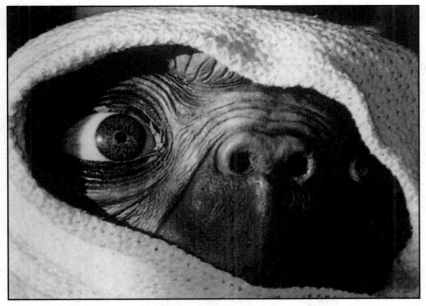

E.T WAS THIS MONKEY FROM OUTER SPACE. AND, LIKE, ALL THESE ASTRONAUT DUDES WANTED TO KILL IT BECAUSE IT HAD A EXTRA TESTICLE, HUH-HUH-HUH! IT'S, LIKE, THEY WERE JELOUS AND STUFF. OH, YEAH, AND THIS MOVIE MADE BEAVIS CRY, HUH-HUH-HUH-HUH!

SHUT-UP, BUTT-HEAD! I WAS CRYING CUZ I LIKE, HAD SOME POPCORN IN MY EYE. BESIDES, IT MADE YOU CRY TOO, BUTT-KNOCKER!

NO WAY! I WAS CRYING CUZ, UHH, I WAS SAD TO SEE THAT YOU WERE SUCH A WUSS, HUH-HUH.

CHECK IT OUT, HEH-HEH. THIS IS THAT PART WHERE THE OTHER ALIEN DUDES ARE LIKE, "LET'S DITCH THAT E.T DUDE. HEH-HEH. HE SUCKS."

YEAH, HUH-HUH. SOMETIMES, E.T'S STOMACH STARTED BURNING UP. HEH-HEH. IT WAS ALL, LIKE, RED. I THINK HE HAD A ULCER OR SOMETHING. LIKE, HANGING AROUND THAT STUPID ELIOT KID JUST MADE IT WORSE, HUH-HUH.

WHEN THAT KID CUT HIS FINGER E.T.'D GO "OUUUCH" AND TOUCH THE KID'S FINGER AND THEN THE KID WAS OKAY. HEH-HEH! IF ME AND E.T HUNG OUT, I'D, LIKE, JUMP INTO A VOLCANO WITH SOME DYNAMITE STRAPPED ON ME AND JUST BEFORE I HIT THE LAVA, I'D BLOW MYSELF UP AND THEN MY BODY PARTS WOULD GET ALL BURNED UP IN THE LAVA, HEH-HEH-HEH. AND THEN E.T'D TOUCH ME AND I'D BE OKAY AGAIN, HEH-HEH. IT WOULD RULE!

ALIEN AUTOPSY

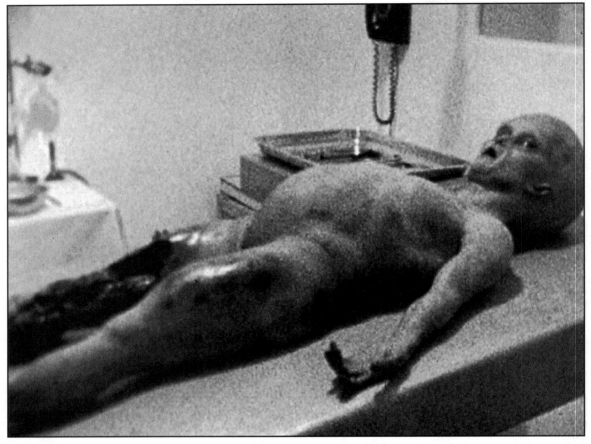

THERE WAS THIS COOL TV SHOW THAT WAS, LIKE, FOR REAL, WHERE A COUPLE OF SCIENTIFIC DUDES GOT THIS DEAD ALIEN AND STARTED CHOPPING ITS GUTS OUT! HEH-HEH-HEH! IT RULED!

YEAH, HUH-HUH-HUH. EVERYONE KEPT ASKING IF IT WAS REAL AND STUFF. BUT LIKE, IF IT WASN'T REAL, IT WOULDN'T HAVE BEEN ON TV.

THESE DUDES THAT CUT UP THE ALIEN DIDN'T DO IT RIGHT. THIS IS WHAT ME AND BEAVIS THINK THEY SHOULD'VE DONE:

THEY SHOULD'VE TURNED THE ALIEN OVER AND LOOKED AT ITS BUTT, HUH-HUH-HUH!

THEY SHOULD'VE STUCK ITS FINGER IN ITS NOSE, SO IT LOOKED LIKE THE ALIEN WAS PICKING IT, HEH-HEH-HEH!

AFTER THEY CUT IT OPEN ONE DUDE SHOULD'VE CLIMBED INSIDE IT, AND LIKE, CRAWLED AROUND INSIDE THE ALIEN FOR AWHILE. THEN HE SHOULD'VE STUCK HIS HEAD OUT ITS BUTT AND WENT "PEEK-A-BOO!"

THEY SHOULD'VE CUT ITS HEAD OFF, THEN FLUSHED IT DOWN THE TOILET, HUH-HUH-HUH!

THEY SHOULD'VE PUT ITS HAND ON ITS SCHLONG, SO IT LOOKED LIKE IT WAS CHOKING ITS CHICKEN! HEH-HEH-HEH!

THEY SHOULD'VE STUFFED A BUNCH OF GARBAGE IN ITS MOUTH THEN JUMP UP AND DOWN ON ITS STOMACH AND LIKE, WATCH ALL THE CRAP SHOOT OUT OF ITS MOUTH.

ONE OF THEM SHOULD'VE MADE THE ALIENS MOUTH MOVE AND SAY "I SUCK" AND "I'M A DORK." HUH-HUH-HUH! AND "I CRASHED THE UFO CUZ I WAS DRUNK."

THE TOOTH FAIRY

Me and Beavis wanted to prove if there really was a Tooth Fairy. Huh-huh. We had a plan, or something. So, like, first we needed some teeth, huh-huh-huh. Beavis' teeth. Huh-huh-huh-huh.

Then we put Beavis' teeth under the pillow. He was gonna pretend to be sleeping and I was gonna hide under the bed, and so, like, when the Tooth Fairy came by, I was gonna jump up and spray bug spray on it, huh-huh!

Yeah, heh-heh-heh-heh! And then we were gonna sell it to the pet store. I bet we'd get, like, five bucks for it! Heh-heh-heh.

But then, umm, I fell asleep for real and I had a "nocturnal mission." Heh-heh-heh-heh!

Beavis, you butt-munch, you messed up the plan.

Oh, yeah, heh-heh. I messed-up the bed, too. Heh-heh-hmm-heh-heh

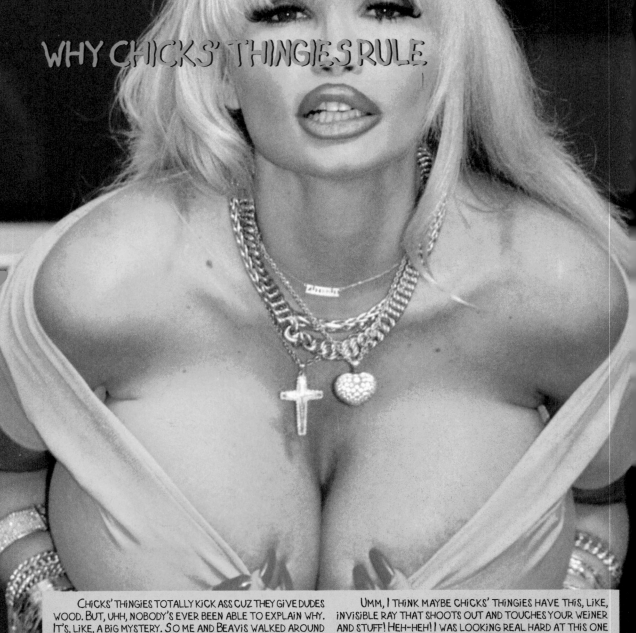

WHY CHICKS' THINGIES RULE.

CHICKS' THINGIES TOTALLY KICK ASS CUZ THEY GIVE DUDES WOOD. BUT, UHH, NOBODY'S EVER BEEN ABLE TO EXPLAIN WHY. IT'S, LIKE, A BIG MYSTERY. SO ME AND BEAVIS WALKED AROUND AND LOOKED AT CHICKS' THINGIES AND GOT STIFFYS, ALL IN THE NAME OF SCIENCE OR SOMETHING. HUH-HUH-HUH.

HERE'S SOME IDEAS WE GOT FROM THE EXPEARMINT ABOUT WHY THINGIES GIVE DUDES STIFFYS:

UMM, CHICKS' THINGIES JIGGLE, KINDA LIKE A DUDE'S NADS! SO WHEN A DUDE SEES JIGGLY THINGIES IT REMINDS HIM OF HIS NADS! HEH-HEH! AND SO THE DUDE'S, LIKE, "OHHH, YEAH. I'VE GOT NADS. THAT RULES!"

I THINK THINGIES GIVE DUDES STIFFYS CUZ THINGIES KINDA LOOK LIKE A BUTT THAT'S ON THE CHICKS' STOMACH. HUH-HUH-HUH! THAT'S COOL!

UMM, I THINK MAYBE CHICKS' THINGIES HAVE THIS, LIKE, INVISIBLE RAY THAT SHOOTS OUT AND TOUCHES YOUR WEINER AND STUFF! HEH-HEH! I WAS LOOKING REAL HARD AT THIS ONE CHICK'S THINGIES AT THE MALL AND I SAW A INVISIBLE RAY OR SOMETHING SHOOT OUT OF HER THINGIES RIGHT AT MY WEINER. HEH-HEH! THEN, LIKE, A SECOND LATER MY WEINER FELT SPE-CIAL! HEH-HEH-HEH! BOIiiiING!

CHICK'S THINGIES USE, UHH, MENTAL TELEPATHY OR SOME-THING TO TALK TO YOUR WEINER. WHEN THINGIES SEE A DUDE THEY'RE LIKE, "HEY, WEINER. HOW'S IT GOING? LET'S PARTY." AND THE DUDE'S WEINER IS KINDA LIKE A ANTENNA OR SOMETHING. HUH-HUH-HUH! IT HAS TO, YOU KNOW, STAND AT ATTENTION SO IT CAN, LIKE, PICK-UP THE MESSAGES THE THINGIES ARE SENDING. HUH-HUH-HUH-HUH!

THIS WOULD BE THE COOLEST SCI-FI MOVIE OF ALL TIME. HUH-HUH. NOTHING WOULD EVER BE COOLER.

Deep in the Arctic, they hunt their prey. They're big. They're soft. They're... terrifying! Can any man survive the horror of...

THE THINGIES

A REALLY COOL PRODUCTION
STARRING ANNA NICOLE SMITH'S BOOBS, THE GUY FROM "ESCAPE FROM L.A." AND BUTT-HEAD AS THE EXPERT ON THINGIES. SPECIAL EFFECTS SUPERVISOR AND GRIP: BEAVIS.

UHH, THIS MOVIE HAD SOME REALLY COOL DIALOG AND STUFF. HERE'S SOME OF THE BEST LINES:

"GENTLEMEN, AFTER MUCH SCIENTIFIC STUDY, I HAVE DETERMINED THAT THEY ARE A GARGANTUAN SET OF MAMMARY GLANDS, HUH-HUH-HUH. IN OTHER WORDS, A HUGE PAIR OF BOOBS."

"LOOK, THE COLD AIR IS DOING SOMETHING TO THEM!"

"WHOA! HUH-HUH-HUH! COME TO BUTT-HEAD!"

"IF WE COULD ONLY HARNESS THEIR POWER, WE COULD FEED THE ENTIRE WORLD!"

"I'D LIKE TO GET A CLOSER LOOK, UH-HUH-HUH, FOR, UH, SCIENTIFIC REASONS."

"DON'T GET BETWEEN THEM! IT'S, LIKE, SUICIDE OR SOMETHING!"

"THE POOR THINGIE EXPERT NEVER HAD A CHANCE. THE THINGIES SMOTHERED HIM, THEN CRUSHED HIM TO DEATH. IT MUST HAVE BEEN A TERRIBLE WAY TO DIE. BUT LOOK AT HIS FACE...IT ALMOST LOOKS LIKE HE'S SMILING."

TWILIGHT ZONE

THERE'S THIS PLACE CALLED THE TWILIGHT ZONE WHERE THINGS THAT SUCK HAPPEN TO YOU. AND THERE'S THIS DUDE THAT HANGS OUT THERE, SMOKING AND SAYING STUFF THAT DOESN'T MAKE ANY SENSE. ONE TIME, ME AND BUTT-HEAD GOT TRAPPED IN THE TWILIGHT ZONE FOR A WHILE, AND IT SUCKED! CHECK IT OUT

VAN DREISSEN: BEAVIS AND BUTT-HEAD! DON'T YOU @#$% KNOW THAT CLASS BEGINS AT OH-NINE-HUNDRED SHARP?! IT'S 9:01! GET IN YOUR SEATS BEFORE I BREAK YOUR *&#@% NECKS!

BUTT-HEAD: OH, MY GOODNESS! MR. VAN DREISSEN IS QUITE ANGRY. IT FRIGHTENS ME WHEN HE USES SUCH FOUL LANGUAGE.

BEAVIS: HEH-HEH-HEH, WHY BUTT-HEAD, YOU JUST SPOKE IN THE MOST UNUSUAL MANNER. IT WAS QUITE ODD! OH, DEAR! I AM SPEAKING IN THE SAME ERUDITE FASHION!

IMAGINE, IF YOU WILL, TWO TYPICAL, UNDERACHIEVING HIGH SCHOOL BOYS HAVING A DAY THAT'S ANYTHING BUT ORDINARY. BECAUSE WHEN BEAVIS AND BUTT-HEAD ENTERED THEIR CLASSROOM, THEY ALSO STEPPED INTO... THE TWILIGHT ZONE.

BUTT-HEAD: MY NAME "BUTT-HEAD" IS SO VERY CRUDE AND OFFENSIVE. I BELIEVE I WILL CHANGE IT TO THE MORE PROPER GLUTEUS MAXIMUS-HEAD.

STEWART: I'M GONNA CUT YOUR GUTS OUT IF YOU DON'T GIVE ME ALL YOUR MONEY.

BEAVIS: DON'T WORRY GLUTEUS MAXIMUS-HEAD, MY STALWART COMPANION. I WOULD PROTECT YOU WITH MY VERY LIFE. AND AS FOR YOU, STEWART, KNIVES ARE DANGEROUS. AND FURTHERMORE, THEY ARE NOT ALLOWED IN CLASS.

DARIA: SO, GUYS, YOU WANNA MEET M[E]
AT MY PLACE AFTER SCHOOL? WE'LL,
LIKE, GET DRUNK AND DO IT ALL NIGH[T]
LONG! HEY, I THINK I CAN SEE YOUR
WEINERS, HAW-HAW-HAW! THAT'S
COOL!

BUTT-HEAD: DARIA, SOME OF US
ARE HERE TO LEARN, NOT TO BE
DISTRACTED BY YOUR JUVENILE
COMMENTS AND OFFENSIVE BEHAVIO[R]

BEAVIS: AND AS FOR YOUR PROPOSI-
TION OF A SEXUAL TRYST, I, FOR ONE,
AM CERTAINLY NOT INTERESTED, YOU
VILE STRUMPET. PREMARITAL SEX IS
SIMPLY WRONG.

BUZZCUT: I HAVE WONDERFUL NEWS
FOR YOU, BOYS. YOUR HARD WORK AND
SUPERIOR STUDY HABITS HAVE PAID OF[F]
YOU'VE BEEN ACCEPTED TO OXFORD
UNIVERSITY ON A FULL SCHOLARSHIP.
I WILL TRULY MISS YOU.

BEAVIS: WHAT JOYOUS NEWS! OUR
DREAMS AND ASPIRATIONS HAVE COM[E]
TRUE!

BUTT-HEAD: COME WITH US TO
COLLEGE, MR. BUZZCUT! YOU ARE OU[R]
FRIEND AND WE LOVE YOU.

AND SO, A VERY
UNUSUAL SCHOOL DAY
COMES TO AN END, IN A VERY
UNUSUAL CLASS ROOM
LOCATED SOMEWHERE IN
THE FAR CORNERS OF...
THE TWILIGHT ZONE.

BUTT-HEAD: THAT GENTLEMAN'S
NAME IS ROD. WHAT A FINE NAME!

CONTACTING DEAD PEOPLE

ME AND BUTT-HEAD WANTED TO TALK TO SOME GHOSTS OF DEAD PEOPLE. THE WAY YOU DO IT IS, YOU, LIKE, SIT IN A DARK ROOM AND LIGHT A CANDLE AND THINK OF DEAD PEOPLE. HEH-HEH! BUT, UMM, YOU GOTTA, LIKE, HOLD HANDS OR SOMETHING.

YEAH. THAT BUTT-KNOCKER BEAVIS TRIED TO HOLD MY HAND, SO I KICKED THE LIVING CRAP OUT OF HIM. HUH-HUH-HUH! AND WHILE I WAS BEATING ON BEAVIS A BUNCH OF DEAD DUDES SHOWED UP ANYWAY, HUH-HUH-HUH! THIS IS, LIKE, WHAT THEY SAID:

BEAVIS: WHOA! IT'S SOME OLD DUDE! HEH-HEH!

OLD DUDE: FINALLY! I HAVE BEEN TRYING TO CONTACT THE LIVING FOR SO LONG! I AM ALBERT EINSTEIN. IN DEATH I HAVE LEARNED OF SO MANY WONDERFUL THINGS! SIMPLE ANSWERS TO MYSTERIES THAT HAVE PUZZLED MAN FOR AGES. I CAN TELL YOU IF THERE IS A GOD, OR IF THERE IS LIFE ON OTHER PLANETS. I CAN EVEN TELL YOU THE MEANING OF LIFE! NOW, DO YOU HAVE ANY QUESTIONS?

BUTT-HEAD: UHH, WHAT'S IT LIKE TO SCORE?

BEAVIS: AND, UMM, WHICH EPISODE OF XENA: WARRIOR PRINCESS IS ON TONIGHT? HEH-HEH!

BEAVIS: CHECK IT OUT! SOME AINCHENT DUDE FROM THE 60'S. HEH-HEH!

AINCHENT DUDE: I AM NOSTRODOMUS. LISTEN CAREFULLY! I SHALL REVEAL WHEN AND WHERE TERRIBLE CALAMITIES WILL STRIKE EARTH WITHIN THE NEXT YEARS. WITH THIS KNOWLEDGE YOU MAY SPREAD THE NEWS AND BE ABLE TO SAVE UNTOLD MILLIONS OF LIVES FROM DISASTER.

BUTT-HEAD: YOU SAID "SPREAD." HUH-HUH-HUH!

BEAVIS: WHOA! IT'S BRUCE LEE! HEH-HEH-HEH! HEY, MAN, HOW'S IT GOIN'?

BRUCE LEE: PRETTY GOOD.

BEAVIS: THAT ONE MOVIE WHERE YOU KICKED LIKE, A HUNDRED ASSES RULED, HEH-HEH-HEH! AND THAT TIME YOU PUNCHED THAT BIG GUY IN THE BUTT! HYAAAA! PLOP! HEH-HEH!

BUTT-HEAD: HEY, BRUCE. WE SHOULD HANG OUT, CUZ, YOU KNOW, I LIKE TO KICK DUDE'S ASSES, TOO. HUH-HUH-HUH. IN FACT, I WAS JUST KICKING BEAVIS' ASS. CHECK IT OUT. I'M GONNA DO IT AGAIN.

BEAVIS: NO WAY, BUTT-HEAD! OWW! CUT IT OUT, FART-KNOCKER! AGGGH!

PEOPLE WHO, LIKE, ALL OF A SUDDEN BURN UP FOR NO REASON

CHECK THIS OUT! THERE'S SOME PEOPLE WHO, LIKE, ALL OF A SUDDEN BURN-UP, HEH-HEH-HEH, FOR NO REASON! IT'S, LIKE, THEY'RE JUST WALKING AROUND AND ALL OF SUDDEN THEY'RE LIKE, "AUUGGGHH! I'M ON FIRE!" HEH-HEH-HEH! AND THERE'S NOTHING LEFT BUT THEIR SHOES AND A LITTLE PILE OF DIRT! SCIENTIFIC DUDES CALL IT SPOTANUS HUMAN COMBUSTSHUN OR SOMETHING. HEH-HEH-HEH!

SO LIKE, I WAS IN CLASS TRYING TO MAKE MYSELF SPOTANUSLY HUMAN COMBUST AND STUFF. I WAS TRYING LIKE REALLY HARD, HEH-HEH! AND, LIKE, AFTER A FEW HOURS I BLACKED OUT! HEH-HEH-HEH-HEH! SO IT WAS STILL PRETTY COOL!

UMM, YOU PROBABLY THINK IT WOULD SUCK TO ALL OF A SUDDEN BURN UP FOR NO REASON. BUT SOMETIMES IT MIGHT BE COOL. LIKE, FOR EXAMPUL:

IT'D BE COOL IF YOU'RE STANDING AROUND TALKING TO CHICKS AND ONE OF THEM PUT A CIGARETTE IN HER MOUTH. THEN ALL OF A SUDDEN YOU COMBUSTED,

HEH-HEH-HEH! SHE COULD LIGHT HER CIGARETTE ON YOUR HEAD. HEH-HEH! THAT'D BE PRETTY DAMN SMOOTH.

IT'D BE COOL IF YOU'RE, LIKE, WRESTLING WITH SOME GUY IN GYM CLASS AND ALL OF A SUDDEN YOU BURST INTO FLAMES! HEH-HEH! AND HE, LIKE JUMPS UP AND GOES "AHHH-HGH!" YOU'D WIN FOR SURE!

IF YOU'RE TAKING A TEST AND IT'S REALLY HARD, AND THEN YOU COMBUSTED! HEH-HEH! YOU'D BE, LIKE, "UMM, EXCUSE ME, SIR. I'M ON FIRE." HEH-HEH-HEH!

IF YOU COMBUST WHEN IT'S REALLY COLD OUT. YOU'D BE ALL WARM AND THE CHICKS'LL WANNA STAND CLOSE TO YOU. HEH-HEH!

IF YOU'RE AT WORK, TAKING PEOPLE'S ORDERS AND YOUR FACE SUDDENLY BURNS OFF. IT'D FREAK OUT THE CUSTOMERS AND THEY'D PROBA-BLY GO EAT SOMEWHERE ELSE! HEH-HEH-HEH!

IF YOU'RE STANDING IN LINE FOR THE BATHROOM AND YOU SUDDENLY STARTED BURNING UP, PEOPLE WILL PROBABLY BE LIKE, "IT'S OKAY, MAN, I DON'T HAVE TO GO THAT BAD. YOU GO FIRST."

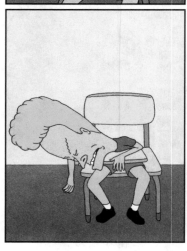

READING PALMS

THERE'S THIS PLACE, OVER BY THE PAWN SHOP AND THE PORN THEATRE. WHEN YOU GO THERE, YOU PAY FIVE BUCKS AND THIS MYSTERIOUS OLD CHICK THAT HAS A LOT OF NECKLACES AND JUNK WILL, LIKE, READ YOUR PALM. AND IT'S PRETTY COOL CUZ SHE CAN TELL YOU WHEN YOU'RE GONNA DIE AND IF YOU'RE GONNA SCORE AND STUFF JUST BY LOOKING AT THE LINES AND STUFF ON YOUR HAND. BEAVIS WANTED TO GET HIS PALM READ, BUT HE DIDN'T HAVE FIVE BUCKS, SO I DID IT FOR A DOLLAR. HERE'S BEAVIS' PALM AND WHAT I FOUND OUT ABOUT HIM:

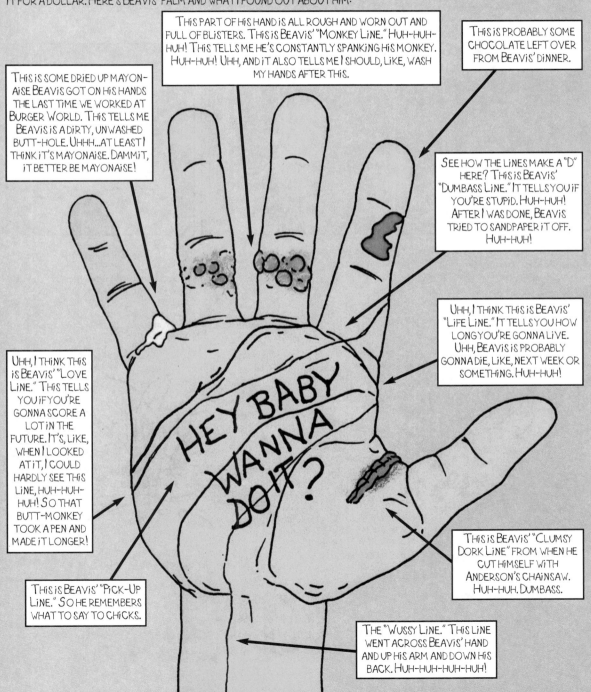

THIS PART OF HIS HAND IS ALL ROUGH AND WORN OUT AND FULL OF BLISTERS. THIS IS BEAVIS' "MONKEY LINE." HUH-HUH-HUH! THIS TELLS ME HE'S CONSTANTLY SPANKING HIS MONKEY. HUH-HUH! UHH, AND IT ALSO TELLS ME I SHOULD, LIKE, WASH MY HANDS AFTER THIS.

THIS IS PROBABLY SOME CHOCOLATE LEFT OVER FROM BEAVIS' DINNER.

THIS IS SOME DRIED UP MAYONAISE BEAVIS GOT ON HIS HANDS THE LAST TIME WE WORKED AT BURGER WORLD. THIS TELLS ME BEAVIS IS A DIRTY, UNWASHED BUTT-HOLE. UHHH...AT LEAST I THINK IT'S MAYONAISE. DAMMIT, IT BETTER BE MAYONAISE!

SEE HOW THE LINES MAKE A "D" HERE? THIS IS BEAVIS' "DUMBASS LINE." IT TELLS YOU IF YOU'RE STUPID. HUH-HUH! AFTER I WAS DONE, BEAVIS TRIED TO SANDPAPER IT OFF. HUH-HUH!

UHH, I THINK THIS IS BEAVIS' "LIFE LINE." IT TELLS YOU HOW LONG YOU'RE GONNA LIVE. UHH, BEAVIS IS PROBABLY GONNA DIE, LIKE, NEXT WEEK OR SOMETHING. HUH-HUH!

UHH, I THINK THIS IS BEAVIS' "LOVE LINE." THIS TELLS YOU IF YOU'RE GONNA SCORE A LOT IN THE FUTURE. IT'S, LIKE, WHEN I LOOKED AT IT, I COULD HARDLY SEE THIS LINE, HUH-HUH-HUH! SO THAT BUTT-MONKEY TOOK A PEN AND MADE IT LONGER!

HEY BABY WANNA DO IT?

THIS IS BEAVIS' "CLUMSY DORK LINE" FROM WHEN HE CUT HIMSELF WITH ANDERSON'S CHAINSAW. HUH-HUH. DUMBASS.

THIS IS BEAVIS' "PICK-UP LINE." SO HE REMEMBERS WHAT TO SAY TO CHICKS.

THE "WUSSY LINE." THIS LINE WENT ACROSS BEAVIS' HAND AND UP HIS ARM AND DOWN HIS BACK. HUH-HUH-HUH-HUH!

GENETIC ENGINE-EARRING

UMM, HEH-HEH, GENETIC ENGINE-EARRING IS WHEN SCIENTIFIC DUDES DO EXPEERMINTS ON ANIMALS. THEY LIKE, PUT EM TOGETHER SCIENTIFICULY AND, LIKE, MAKE BRAND-NEW ANIMALS OUT OF EM, HEH-HEH-HEH.

IN SCHOOL, VAN DRIESSEN WAS TALKING ABOUT HOW, UMM, IN THE FUTURE THERE'S GONNA BE A LOT OF THIS GENETIC ENGINE-EARRING. BUT THEN HE SAID THIS STUFF IS, LIKE, REALLY MESSED-UP AND UNNATURAL OR SOMETHING. SO ME AND BUTT-HEAD WANTED TO TRY IT! HEH-HEH-HEH!

1) FIRST YOU GET TWO BUGS YOU WANNA GENETIC ENGINE-EAR. UMM, HERE WE HAVE A SPIDER AND A WORM, HEH-HEH-HMM.

2) THEN YOU SMASH EM TOGETHER, HEH-HEH-HEH!

3) SEE? HEH-HEH. NOW YOU GOT AN ALL-NEW BUG, HEH-HEH-HEH. THEN YOU HAVE TO NAME WHAT KIND OF A BUG IT IS. SO, UMM, SINCE THIS WAS A SPIDER AND A WORM, THIS'LL BE A...UMM..."SPIRM," HEH-HEH! HEH-HEH-HEH! I'VE GOT "SPIRM" IN MY HANDS, HEH-HEH-HEH-HEH-HEH!

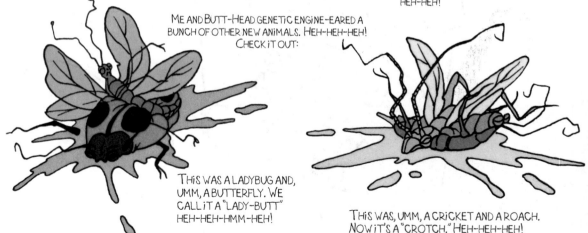

ME AND BUTT-HEAD GENETIC ENGINE-EARED A BUNCH OF OTHER NEW ANIMALS. HEH-HEH-HEH! CHECK IT OUT:

THIS WAS A LADYBUG AND, UMM, A BUTTERFLY. WE CALL IT A "LADY-BUTT" HEH-HEH-HMM-HEH!

THIS WAS, UMM, A CRICKET AND A ROACH. NOW IT'S A "CROTCH." HEH-HEH-HEH!

SOME OF OUR OTHER NEW ANIMALS:
* WE SQUISHED TOGETHER A TERMITE AND A DEAD BIRD. HEH-HEH-HEH! NOW IT'S A "TIRD."
* A DEAD LIZARD AND A DEAD TOAD. WE CALLED IT A "LOAD," HEH-HEH!
* WE MASHED UP A LADYBUG AND A CENTIPEDE. NOW IT'S A "LADY-PEED," HEH-HEH-HEH-HEH!

FAMILIES

Families. Huh-huh-huh.

Families are a mystery cuz it's like when kids hang out with their mom and dad, on purpose. And they, like, do things together, huh-huh-huh! And they're, like, all happy and talking and stuff. What a bunch of dorks! And, uhh, sometimes, the dads live with the family. And they spend "quality time" with their kids. Huh-huh-huh!

Whoa! That's pretty messed up! Heh-heh. It's, like, I feel sorry for them and stuff.

Families suck. Huh-huh. Uhh, nobody knows why, but sometimes you can find a family that's pretty cool. Here's how to tell if your family sucks or if it's cool:

	FAMILIES THAT SUCK	COOL FAMILIES
DADS	One time I heard some kid tell his dad that he loves him, heh-heh-heh! And the dad said "I love you too, son."	Once, I threw a spatula at my mom's boyfriend and he kicked my ass. Heh-heh-heh! He was cool!
MOMS	The mom is always driving the kids everywhere and dropping them off, saying: "Have fun and be careful."	You call your mom to pick you up, and all you hear is a bunch of coughing and then she hangs up.
DINNER	They all eat together and they're always going, "Please pass the potatos." And, uhh, "How was your day?"	You go by yourself and eat a whole bag of marshmallows in the parking lot at Maxi-Mart. Then when you're full you put marshmallows in the street and watch cars run over them, huh-huh-huh!
WHEN SOMEONE DIES	Stewart was crying when his uncle died. Heh-heh!	Umm, when my uncle got shot in prison, they gave me his porn collection. It ruled!
GOING TO BED	The parents are always tucking their kids into bed and saying "sweet dreams." Huh-huh.	You fall asleep on the couch watching TV and your mom and her boyfriend come home drunk and swear at you and tell you to get off the couch so they can do it, huh-huh.

ALIEN ABDUKSHUNS & EXSPEERMINTS ON HUMANS

YOU KNOW HOW PEOPLE ARE ALWAYS ON THOSE TALK SHOWS, SAYING HOW ALIENS TOOK THEM ON THEIR SPACESHIPS AND THEN, YOU KNOW, DID IT WITH THEM? HUH-HUH-HUH. THAT'S WHAT ME AND BEAVIS ARE GONNA DO. WE'RE, LIKE, GONNA WAIT HERE 'TIL SOME ALIENS STEAL US, HUH-HUH, AND DO US, HUH-HUH-HUH-HUH.

WE'RE GONNA SCORE WITH ALIENS, HEH-HEH-HEH! IT'S, LIKE, PROBABLY EASIER THAN SCORING WITH CHICKS ON EARTH. AND IT'S GONNA BE COOL!

YEAH, HUH-HUH. AND SOMETIMES, AFTER ALIENS SCORE WITH YOU, THEY DO EXPEERMINTS ON YOUR, UHH, EQUIPMINT, HUH-HUH-HUH. THESE ARE SOME OF THE EXPEERMINTS ALIENS PROBABLY DO:

* TAKE A BIG DEATH RAY AND BLOW UP YOUR NUT-SACK.

* BEAM YOUR SCHLONG TO ANOTHER TIME.

* THEY TAKE A LIGHT SABER AND FIGHT WITH YOUR WEINER.

* SHOOT A FREEZE BOLT AT YOUR BUTT-CHEEKS.

* MAKE YOUR PUBLIC HAIR RADIOACTIVE SO IT GLOWS IN THE DARK.

* DISINTEGRATE YOUR BUTTHOLE.

* ELECTROCUTE YOUR WEINER TO DEATH.

CLOSE ENCOUNTERS OF THE TURD KIND

This is, like, another movie that would've been cooler if me and Beavis directed it. First, we'd change the name. But, like, you already saw that. Huh-huh. Then we'd make the aliens cool:

And like, we'd change a few scenes. Uh-huh-huh.

STATUES THAT CRY

WE SAW ON TV THAT THERE'S THIS STATUE OF SOME FAMOUS HICK IN SOME CHURCH. AND IT'S SUPPOSED TO CRY. BUT NOBODY KNOWS WHY. SO WE DID OUR OWN INVESTIGASHUN AND CHECKED OUT SOME DIFFERENT STATUES TO SEE IF THEY CRIED TOO.

THIS STATUE WAS IN THE ART MUSEUM. WE KEPT SPITTING ON IT, SO IT'D LOOK LIKE IT WAS CRYING. THEN WE STARTED KICKING IT AND A COP CAME BY AND KICKED US OUTTA THERE. HUH-HUH-HUH!

THIS STATUE DIDN'T CRY. SO WE THOUGHT WE'D MAKE IT CRY. BEAVIS GOT ON TOP OF IT AND STARTED BITING IT REALLY HARD. IT DIDN'T WORK ON THE STATUE, BUT AFTER AWHILE BEAVIS STARTED HOLDING HIS MOUTH AND CRYING. HUH-HUH-HUH!

WE FOUND THIS STATUE IN A STORE. IT DIDN'T CRY EITHER. BUT I HEARD SOMEWHERE THAT SMELLING ONIONS MAKES YOU CRY. SO WE GOT A ONION AND HELD IT UNDER THIS STATUE'S NOSE ALL DAY. IT DIDN'T WORK, SO BEAVIS GOT PISSED AND CRAMMED THE ONION IN THE STATUES NOSE, AND THAT KNOCKED THE STATUE OVER AND IT'S HEAD BROKE OPEN. HUH-HUH-HUH! THEN A LADY WHO WORKED AT THE STORE STARTED CRYING.

THIS CHICK STATUE WAS IN THE PARK. IT DIDN'T CRY, BUT WE TOUCHED HER THINGIES. HUH-HUH-HUH! THEN BEAVIS TOOK OFF HIS PANTS AND STARTED RUBBING UP AGAINST IT. IT WAS COLD OUT AND HIS WEINER GOT STUCK TO THE STATUE, HUH-HUH-HUH-HUH! BEAVIS FREAKED OUT AND STARTED CRYING AGAIN BECAUSE HE THOUGHT HE WAS GONNA BE STUCK FOREVER. HUH-HUH!

REINCARNASHUN

SOME PEOPLE THINK THAT THEY WERE ONCE OTHER PEOPLE IN THE PAST. LIKE IN ANOTHER LIFE AND STUFF. THESE ARE SOME OF THE PEOPLE ME AND BEAVIS USED TO BE IN ANOTHER LIFE:

IN ANOTHER LIFE, ME AND BEAVIS GOT TO DRIVE A BOAT CALLED THE, UHH, TITANIC OR SOMETHING. HUH-HUH. IT HAD A COOL NAME. AT LEAST THE FIRST PART, HUH-HUH!

IN THE 40'S WE RAN SOME RADAR THING JUST BEFORE SOME WAR STARTED OR SOMETHING. IT WAS COOL CUZ WE GOT TO BE IN HAWAII.

THEN, LIKE, IN THE 60'S WE WERE SERVICE DUDES FOR SOME PRESIDENT. I THINK THEY NAMED HIM AFTER THAT ONE ANNOYING CHICK WITH GLASSES THAT'S ON MTV. HUH-HUH. ONE DAY, WE GOT TO HANG OUT AT THIS ONE PARADE IN DALLAS.

BLACK HOLES

UHH, HUH-HUH-HUH. THIS IS, LIKE, A MYSTERY TO SCIENCE DUDES. THEY LIKE, DON'T KNOW WHAT BLACK HOLES ARE OR WHERE THEY ARE. SOME OF THEM EVEN THINK IT'S, LIKE, IN SPACE, HUH-HUH-HUH! THIS IS A PICTURE OF A BLACK HOLE. IF YOU'RE LIKE, SO STUPID THAT YOU STILL DON'T KNOW WHAT THIS IS, HERE'S SOME HINTS OR SOMETHING:

1. SOMETIMES BEAVIS' FINGER GOES THERE.

2. IF YOU, LIKE, DRINK SODA AND LAUGH, THE SODA COMES SHOOTING OUT OF IT.

3. YOU USE IT TO BREATHE.

4. IT GROSSES OUT CHICKS IF YOU STICK FOOD IN IT AND THEN EAT IT.

5. SOMETIMES IF YOU DIG AROUND FOR A WHILE, YOU FIND STUFF IN IT.

6. YOU CAN WALK AROUND WITH PENCILS STUCK IN IT.

7. REALLY COOL PEOPLE GET THIS PIERCED.

ANSWER: A BUTTHOLE, HUH-HUH-HUH! YOU DUMBASS.

THE TERMINATOR

BUTT-HEAD LIKED THIS MOVIE SO MUCH THAT HE TRIED TO COPY IT. HEH-HEH! WHAT A DUMBASS. HEH-HEH!

UHH, I'M A FRIEND OF SARA CONNER, HUH-HUH. CAN I, LIKE, SEE HER?

GET OUT OF HERE, YOU LITTLE MORON. I'M BUSY.

UHH, I'LL BE BACK. HUH-HUH-HUH.

HUH-HUH-HUH. THIS IS GONNA BE COOL. HUH-HUH-HUH.

WHAT THE HELL?

OWW. HUH-HUH.

BIGFOOT

UHH, THIS IS BEAVIS' MOM. HUH-HUH-HUH! AKSHULLY, THIS IS LIKE, SOME WILD DUDE WITH A REALLY BIG FOOT. SOME PEOPLE CALL IT A "SACK-SQUASH," HUH-HUH-HUH! THAT'S CUZ, LIKE, IT KICKS GUYS IN THE NUT-SACK WITH ITS BIG FOOT, HUH-HUH-HUH! THEN BEFORE YOU CAN KICK IT IN THE NADS IN REVENGE, IT RUNS INTO THE WOODS AND HIDES AND PROBABLY, LIKE, LAUGHS ABOUT IT AND STUFF, HUH-HUH-HUH!

OTHER LITTLE-KNOWN BIGFOOT FACTS:

ONE TIME HE FOUGHT THE SIX-MILLION DOLLAR MAN. WE SAW IT ON TV. IT WAS COOL.

HE INVENTED THAT BIG TRUCK WITH THE GIANT WHEELS. HE USED TO DRIVE IT IN THE WOODS, BUT THEN HE NEEDED SOME MONEY SO HE SOLD IT TO SOME GUY AT A MONSTER-TRUCK SHOW.

HOW TO FAKE A BIGFOOT SIGHTING

IT'S LIKE, PRETTY EASY TO TRICK PEOPLE WITH A FAKE BIGFOOT PICTURE THAT YOU CAN SELL FOR LOTS OF MONEY.

TO MAKE A FAKE BIGFOOT PICTURE, YOU NEED TO, LIKE, DO SOME STUFF:

FIRST, YOU GET SOME HAIR. WE BORROWED SOME FROM A POODLE, HUH-HUH-HUH. THEN YOU, LIKE, GLUE IT ON BEAVIS.

AFTER BEAVIS IS ALL HAIRY AND STUFF, MAKE HIM STAND BY A BUSH. HUH-HUH-HUH! UHH, THEN YOU TAKE HIS PICTURE. AND WHEN YOU TRY SELLING THE PICTURE, TELL EVERYONE THAT YOU WERE REALLY SCARED AND STUFF. AND THAT YOU WOULD'VE TAKEN MORE PICTURES, BUT HE KICKED YOU IN THE NADS.

AND ONE MORE THING. YOU NEED SOME BIGFOOT FOOTPRINTS TO PROVE THAT YOU REALLY SAW IT. HERE'S HOW TO MAKE SOME FAKE BIGFOOT FOOTPRINTS:

FIND SOME MUD. THEN, YOU'LL NEED A GIANT FOOT, HUH-HUH. SO LIKE, FIRST, TAKE OFF YOUR SHOE. THEN SMASH YOUR FOOT REALLY HARD WITH A BASEBALL BAT, HUH-HUH-HUH! KEEP SMASHING IT UNTIL YOUR FOOT SWELLS UP BIGGER. THEN WALK AROUND IN THE MUD AND MAKE A BUNCH OF FOOTPRINTS. NOW EVERY-ONE'LL BELIEVE YOU AND YOU CAN SELL THE PICTURE FOR A LOT OF MONEY. HUH-HUH!

SANTA CLAWS

ON CHRISTMAS EVE, SANTA CLAWS GOES AROUND THE WORLD AND GIVES OUT EMPTY BEER CANS AND CIGARETTE BUTTS TO LITTLE KIDS. AT LEAST THAT'S WHAT ME AND BUTT-HEAD ALWAYS GOT, HEH-HEH. CHRISTMAS WAS COOL. BUT, UMM, THERE'S A LOT OF PEOPLE WHO THINK SANTA CLAWS IS LIKE, THIS NICE OLD DUDE WHO LIVES ON A POLE AND WEARS RED PAJAMAS. HEH-HEH. THAT'S LIKE, WRONG. ME AND BUTT-HEAD FOLLOWED SANTA ON CHRISTMAS EVE AND HE DIDN'T KNOW IT. HERE'S SOME SECRET PICTURES WE TOOK:

1. SANTA WAS AT THE MALL AND A BUNCH OF KIDS WERE SITTING ON HIM. LATER, HE WENT IN BACK AND TOOK OFF HIS RED PAJAMAS AND THEN HE, LIKE, RIPPED OFF HIS BEARD. WITHOUT THAT STUFF, YOU COULD SEE HE'S JUST A SWEATY OLD SLOB, HEH-HEH-HEH. INSTEAD OF LOADING UP HIS SACK WITH PRESENTS, HE LOADED UP A PAPER BAG WITH MONEY OUT OF A CASH REGISTER. HEH-HEH! THEN HE TOOK OFF IN A HURRY TO START DELIVERING STUFF TO PEOPLE.

2. SANTA'S SLED MUST'VE BEEN BUSTED OR SOMETHING, CUZ HE RODE OFF ON A BUS. WE SAT BEHIND HIM. HE KEPT TALKING TO HIMSELF AND SWEARING A LOT. IT WAS COOL, HEH-HEH-HEH. THE FIRST PLACE HE STOPPED TO DELIVER PRESENTS WAS A BAR. NOBODY LEFT HIM ANY MILK AND COOKIES, SO THE BARTENDER DUDE GAVE HIM SOME BOOZE AND PRETZELS INSTEAD. SANTA DIDN'T GIVE ANYONE ANYTHING, BUT BEFORE HE LEFT HE PUNCHED SOME GUY. HE MUST'VE BEEN ON SANTA'S "NAUGHTY" LIST, HEH-HEH! THEN SANTA STUMBLED OUTSIDE AND PUKED, HEH-HEH-HEH-HEH!

3. SANTA DOESN'T LIVE ON A POLE, HE LIVES IN A TRAILER PARK. HE HAD LIKE, 10 ELFS THAT LOOKED JUST LIKE KIDS. THEY WEREN'T MAKING TOYS, THEY WERE JUST, LIKE, RUNNING ALL OVER THE PLACE, REFUSING TO GO TO BED AND STUFF. WHEN SANTA CAME HOME FROM THE BAR, HE STARTED SCREAMING AT THE ELFS TO GO TO BED, AND THEN HE SMASHED UP HIS PLACE, HEH-HEH-HEH. THEN MRS. CLAWS CALLED THE COPS AND THEY DRAGGED SANTA TO JAIL. HEH-HEH-HEH-HEH!

HOW CAN SANTA, LIKE, PASS OUT ALL HIS PRESENTS IN ONE NIGHT? WE DID SOME MATH AND STUFF TO FIGURE OUT IF HE COULD REALLY DO IT. CHECK THIS OUT:

SO THERE'S LIKE, MAYBE 100,000 PEOPLE IN THE WORLD. AND THERE'S LIKE, A BUNCH OF HOURS IN A NIGHT. SO TO FIND OUT HOW MUCH TIME SANTA'S GOT, YOU, UHH, TAKE 100,000 AND, UHH, ADD A BUNCH TO THAT:

$$100,000 + A BUNCH = = 100,056$$

HE'S GOT 100,056 MINUTES OR SOMETHING. SO WHEN SANTA DROPS OFF PRESENTS, HE HAS TO GO DOWN THE CHIMNEY AND PUT IT UNDER THE TREE AND THEN CLIMB OUT AGAIN. WE HAD TO KNOW HOW LONG IT TOOK SANTA EACH TIME. SO WE GOT SOME EMPTY BEER CANS AND CIGARETTE BUTTS AND BEAVIS TRIED IT ON ANDERSON'S HOUSE.

FIRST, BEAVIS GOT STUCK IN THE CHIMNEY FOR A HALF HOUR. HUH-HUH-HUH. THEN HE FELL OFF THE ROOF AND SPRAINED HIS BUTT IN 2 PLACES. HUH-HUH-HUH! HE STILL COULDN'T GET IN, SO HE HAD TO BUST THE WINDOW AND THROW THE PRESENTS IN. ANDERSON WOKE UP AND STARTED YELLING THAT HE WAS GONNA CALL 911 OR SOMETHING. THE WHOLE THING TOOK, LIKE, 3 HOURS. SO, LIKE, IF THAT HAPPENS TO SANTA IN EVERY HOUSE IN THE WORLD, THAT WOULD BE, UHH...

$$2 + 911 + 3 = 29,113$$
$$THE DIVIDE 29,113 INTO 2 = 29 AND 113$$

IT'D TAKE SANTA 29 HOURS AND 113 MINUTES. BUT IF YOU DON'T BELIEVE IN SANTA, HE STOPS AT YOUR HOUSE AND LOOKS IN YOUR WINDOW AND FLIPS YOU OFF. HUH-HUH. WHEN WE TRIED IT WITH STEWART'S HOUSE, IT TOOK BEAVIS, LIKE, 8 SECONDS TO WALK UP TO A WINDOW, LOOK INSIDE AND FLIP SOMEONE OFF. STEWART'S DAD WAS PISSED, HUH-HUH-HUH.

SO, UHH, IF THERE'S LIKE 300 PEOPLE THAT DON'T BELIEVE IN SANTA. AND IF IT TOOK SANTA 8 SECONDS TO FLIP THEM OFF EVERY TIME, THAT WOULD BE, UHH, HMM...

$$300 + 8 = 380.$$

UHH, THEN YOU TAKE THE 100,056 HOURS AND, UHHH, YOU DO SOMETHING WITH IT. I THINK YOU ADD THE 29 HOURS. OR MAYBE THE 380. UHHH...DAMN IT, I'M GETTING SICK OF ALL THIS MATH. IT PROBABLY EQUALS, LIKE, 600 OR SOMETHING. HUH-HUH-HUH. THE END.

CONCLOOSHUN: UHH, THIS PROVES THAT SANTA CAN PASS OUT SOME OF HIS PRESENTS IN ONE NIGHT BUT AFTER THAT HE PROBABLY GETS TIRED AND GOES HOME TO DO IT WITH MRS. CLAWS.

OH, YEAH, AND SANTA IS REAL. IF YOU DON'T BELIEVE IN HIM YOU'LL GO TO HELL. HUH-HUH-HUH.

BAYWATCH NIGHTS

BAYWATCH RULES! IT'S LIKE, IF I EVER MISSED AN EPISODE OF BAYWATCH, FOR THE WHOLE WEEK I'D BE PISSED. BUT THEN THEY MADE ANOTHER SHOW CALLED BAYWATCH NIGHTS. SO WHEN I HEARD ABOUT THAT, I HAD A STIFFY FOR A WEEK. HEH-HEH-HMM-HEH! THEN IT CAME ON AND IT SUCKED! IT WAS SUPPOSED TO BE LIKE, PAMELA ANDERSON AND THE OTHER HOT CHICKS FROM BAYWATCH, EXCEPT AT NIGHT, WHEN THEY GET NAKED AND DO IT! YEEEEAH! HEH-HEH-HEH! BUT, UMM, INSTEAD THE WHOLE SHOW WAS ABOUT THAT FLABBY OLD BUNGHOLE, DAVID HASSELHOFF. HE WAS, LIKE, TRYING TO BE LIKE THAT DUDE FROM X-FILES SOLVING ALL THESE SUPPERNATURAL THINGS. WE DIDN'T SEE ANY CHICKS IN BIKINIS, OR EVEN PAMELA ANDERSON! AND ALL THE CHICKS WEAR REGULAR CLOTHES, DAMMIT! AND THERE'S HARDLY ANY SUPPERNATURAL STUFF! BUT, UMM, DAVID HASSELHOFF HAS BOOBS. HEH-HEH! SO I GUESS THAT'S KINDA SUPPERNATURAL. HEH-HEH-HEH!

ME AND BUTT-HEAD WROTE TO THE PEOPLE AT BAYWATCH TO GIVE THEM SOME IDEAS FOR NEW EPISODES:

PAMELA ANDERSON GETS POSSESSED AND FLOATS AROUND NAKED. AND THE REST OF THE EPISODE TURNS INTO ONE OF THOSE LONG MUSIC VIDEO SCENES, WITH ALL THESE SLOW MOTION SHOTS OF HER BUTT!

PAMELA ANDERSON HAS TO FIGHT A GIGANTIC SCHLONG. HEH-HEH! YEAH. HEH-HEH. MINE.

DAVID HASSELHOFF'S BUTT-HAIR COMES TO LIFE AND JUMPS IN HIS EYES WHILE HE'S DRIVING AND HE WRECKS THE CAR. HEH-HEH-HEH!

A GHOST TRIPS DAVID HASSELHOFF AND HE FALLS DOWN SOME STAIRS AND BREAKS HIS BUNGHOLE. HEH-HEH. THAT WOULD BE COOL!

MOVING AND BREAKING STUFF WITH YOUR BRAIN

UMM, WE LEARNED ON TV THAT SOME PEOPLE HAVE THIS COOL MAGIC POWER, CALLED TELEKINEESIS OR SOMETHING. THEY CAN LIKE, MOVE AND BREAK STUFF WITH THEIR BRAIN, HEH-HEH-HEH. LIKE THIS ONE GUY STARED AT A SPOON AND THEN IT BENT AND THEN BROKE! HEH-HEH! I TRIED STARING AT BUTT-HEAD SO I COULD BEND HIM AND BREAK HIM, BUT HE PUNCHED ME IN THE FACE.

TELEKINEESIS IS PRETTY EASY TO DO. YOU JUST, LIKE, STARE AT SOMETHING AND CONSENTRATE FOR A LONG TIME, AND THIS BIG BLUE VEIN STARTS PUFFING UP ON YOUR FOREHEAD, AND THEN ALL THIS COOL STUFF HAPPENS. HERE'S SOME OF THE THINGS I DID WITH TELEKINEESIS:

* ONE TIME, MY FREEZY WHIP WAS REAL ICY, AND IT WOULDN'T GO UP THE STRAW. SO, I STARED AT IT REAL HARD TO MAKE IT MELT. IT, LIKE, TOOK AWHILE, BUT THEN IT REALLY DID MELT!

* THIS OTHER TIME, AT BURGER WORLD, THIS DUMBASS CUSTOMER WAS ASKING ME ALL THESE QUESTIONS, SO I LIKE, USED MY POWER TO MAKE HIM GO AWAY. AND IT WORKED, CUZ AFTER I STARED AT HIM FOR FIVE MINUTES, HE LEFT!

* AT THE GROCERY STORE, I DIDN'T FEEL LIKE OPENING THE DOOR WITH MY HANDS, SO I JUST USED MY BRAIN. I WAS STARING AT THE DOOR FOR A LONG TIME, BUT IT DIDN'T WORK. I MUST'VE BEEN TOO FAR AWAY, CUZ WHEN I WALKED UP A LITTLE CLOSER TO THE DOOR IT OPENED ALL BY ITSELF RIGHT AWAY! A LOT OF OTHER PEOPLE GOT THE SAME IDEA AS ME, CUZ I SAW THEM OPENING THE DOOR WITH THEIR BRAINS, TOO.

* ONE TIME, PRINCIPAL MCVICKER ASKED ME A QUESTION, BUT I DIDN'T KNOW THE ANSWER, SO I JUST STARED AT HIM FOR LIKE TEN MINUTES. HE DIDN'T BREAK APART, BUT HE STARTED SHAKING REAL BAD AND HE SCREAMED AT ME TO STOP IT. HEH-HEH. I THINK HE'S SCARED OF ME.

* I WANTED IT TO BE NIGHT SO XENA: WARRIOR PRINCESS WOULD COME ON. SO I WAS STARING AT THE SUN, TRYING TO MAKE IT GO DOWN. AFTER AWHILE, I GOT DIZZY AND ALL OF A SUDDEN IT GOT REALLY, REALLY DARK! I WAS LIKE, "COOL! IT WORKED!" AND I STARTED WALKING AROUND BUMPING INTO THINGS. I MEAN, IT WAS REALLY DARK. IT WAS NIGHT FOR A FEW DAYS AND NOBODY TURNED ON ANY LIGHTS AND I COULDN'T FIND MY WAY HOME. THEN I THINK A CAR HIT ME AND SOMEONE TOOK ME TO THE HOSPITAL AND I HAD A OPERATION ON MY EYES. HEH-HEH. NOW I'M OKAY. BUT I THINK I'M GONNA WAIT AWHILE BEFORE I TRY THAT AGAIN.

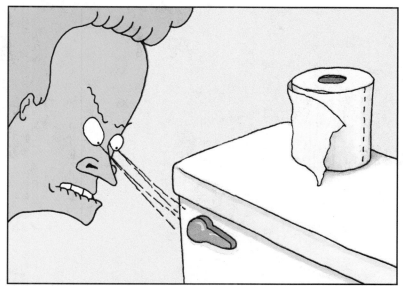

MOVING AND BREAKING STUFF WITH YOUR BRAIN (CONT'D.) THERE WAS A PRETTY COOL MOVIE CALLED CARRIE, ABOUT THIS CHICK THAT USED TELEKINEESIS. EVERYONE MADE FUN OF HER AND LAUGHED AT HER AND STUFF. ONE DAY, SHE WAS AT THIS DANCE AND SOME PEOPLE REALLY PISSED HER OFF. SO THEN SHE STARED AT STUFF AND USED HER BRAIN TO GET BACK AT EVERYONE. HEH-HEH-HEH! IT RULED! IF SOMETHING LIKE THAT HAPPENED TO ME, I'D USE TELEKINEESIS TO GET REVENGE TOO. CHECK IT OUT, HEH-HEH-HEH.

CROP CIRCLES

FARMERS ARE ALWAYS FINDING THESE GIANT THINGS CALLED CROP CIRCLES IN THEIR FIELDS. ALIENS COME DOWN IN THE MIDDLE OF THE NIGHT AND DO THESE JUST TO FREAK PEOPLE OUT. HUH-HUH. ME AND BEAVIS MADE OUR OWN CROP CIRCLE TO FOOL MR. ANDERSON. HE'S GONNA LOOK AT IT AND GO, "WHOA! AN ALIEN MUST'VE DONE THIS!" AND THEN HE'LL POOP IN HIS PANTS, HUH-HUH-HUH!

HOW TO SPOT AN ALIEN

UHH, THERE'S THESE PEOPLE THAT THINK ALIENS ARE RUNNING AROUND ON EARTH, LIKE, DISGUISED AS HUMANS. ME AND BEAVIS LOOKED AT THIS PICTURE OF A REAL ALIEN, AND THEN WE, LIKE, TRIED TO FIND SOME UNDERCOVER ONES. WE LOOKED IN SOME MAGAZINES AND FIGURED OUT THAT THERE'S A LOT OF ALIENS THAT PRETEND TO BE THESE CHICKS CALLED SUPERMODELS. SO IF YOU SEE A SUPERMODEL, YOU SHOULD START POINTING AT HER AND SCREAMING FOR HER TO GO BACK TO HER OWN PLANET AND LEAVE US THE HELL ALONE.

OR, UMM, YOU CAN TELL THE SUPERMODEL THAT YOU WON'T TURN HER IN IF SHE LETS YOU TOUCH HER BOOBS. HEH-HEH-HEH!

OUR PROOF:

HEAD: ALIENS HAVE REALLY BIG HEADS. HUH-HUH. JUST LIKE SUPERMODELS. SUPERMODELS' HEADS ARE HUGE, EVEN THOUGH THEIR BRAINS ARE PRETTY SMALL. HUH-HUH. THEY'RE DUMB.

HAIR: UHH, ALIENS ARE REALLY BALD IN REAL LIFE. SO WHEN THEY DISGUISE THEMSELVES LIKE SUPERMODELS THEY WEAR WIGS. IF YOU SEE A SUPERMODEL, PULL HER WIG OFF. IT MIGHT BE ON KINDA TIGHT BUT KEEP PULLING. HUH-HUH.

NECK: ALIENS AND SUPERMODELS HAVE THESE REALLY LONG, FREAKY-LOOKING STRETCHED OUT NECKS.

EYES: ALIENS AND SUPERMODELS HAVE REAL BIG EYES THAT GIVE OUT DEATH-RAY STARES.

BODY: ALIENS AND SUPERMODELS BOTH HAVE THESE WEAK, SKINNY LITTLE ARMS AND BODIES. I THINK IT'S CUZ EARTH FOOD MAKES THEM SICK OR SOMETHING.

SKIN: ALIENS AND SUPERMODELS HAVE REALLY WHITE SKIN. LIKE THEY'RE SICK OR SOMETHING OR ALWAYS PUKING.

UHH...WAIT A MINUTE. YOU CAN SAY SOME OF THIS STUFF ABOUT BEAVIS, TOO. UHHH...LET ME SEE IF YOUR HAIR IS REAL, BEAVIS. HUH-HUH-HUH!

OWW! HEY, WHAT THE HELL? QUIT PULLING MY HAIR, BUTT-HEAD! AGGGH! STOP IT, FARTKNOCKER!

THE GIANT FLOATING BUTT OF HIGHLAND HIGH

THERE'S THIS BIG BUTT THAT FLOATS AROUND OUR SCHOOL SOMETIMES. I THINK IT ONLY COMES OUT DURING FULL MOONS. HUH-HUH. IT'S, LIKE, YOU'LL BE SITTING IN CLASS AND ALL OF A SUDDEN YOU'LL LOOK UP AND THERE'S THIS GIANT GHOSTLY BUTT THAT FLOATS ACROSS THE ROOM REAL SLOW. THEN IT CUTS THE CHEESE AND DISAPPEARS, HUH-HUH-HUH-HUH!

SOME PEOPLE THINK IT COMES FROM THIS KID, WHO, LIKE, YEARS AND YEARS AGO CUT OFF HIS BUTT IN WOOD SHOP. HUH-HUH-HUH! THE KID LIVED AND STUFF, BUT HIS BUTT DIED. AND NOW THE GHOST OF HIS BUTT HAUNTS HIGHLAND FOREVER, OR SOMETHING.

STAR TREK

UMM, STAR TREK WAS THIS SHOW WHERE THESE DUDES IN THEIR PAJAMAS FLY AROUND IN SPACE AND FIGHT STATIC CLING OR SOMETHING. OR MAYBE IT WAS SOME GUY NAMED KLINGER. HEH-HEH. BUTT-HEAD IS SUCH A DILLHOLE, I BET IF HE WAS IN STAR TREK, HE'D PROBABLY BE LIKE THIS, HEH-HEH:

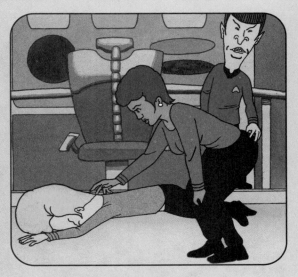

CAPTAIN'S LOG, STARDATE 6969. HEH-HEH-HEH! "LOG"-AGGGH!

THIS VULCAN DEATH GRIP IS COOL, HUH-HUH! SO, LIKE, NOW I'M THE CAPTAIN. I'M GONNA GO TO THE BATH-ROOM AND MAKE A CAPTAIN'S LOG, HUH-HUH-HUH.

WHAT HAPPENED TO THE CAPTAIN?!

UH-HUH-HUH. HEY, BABY. NICE BUTT. WANNA GO DO IT?

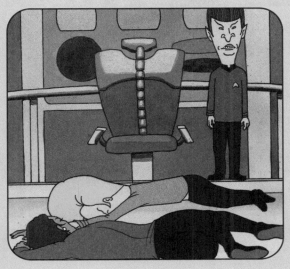

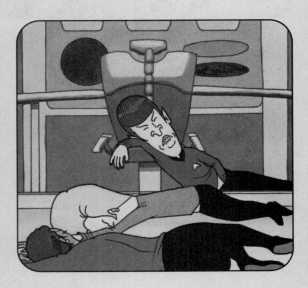

WHOA, HUH-HUH-HUH. SORRY. UHH, I GUESS I'LL JUST HAVE TO, UH-HUH-HUH, SPANK THE MONKEY.

WHY THE BEATLES ARE POPULAR EVEN THOUGH THEY'RE DEAD (AND SUCK)

IT'S, LIKE, A BIG ENOUGH MYSTERY WHY THE BEATLES WERE EVER POPULAR. BUT, LIKE, IT'S EVEN A BIGGER MYSTERY WHY THEY'RE POPULAR NOW THAT THEY'RE DEAD. UHH, THE BEATLES WERE JUST THESE WUSSY DORKS FROM ENGLAND AND THEY DID A BUNCH OF CRAPPY SONGS THAT SUCKED. OLD PEOPLE LIKE THE BEATLES CUZ WHEN THEY WERE LITTLE THERE WASN'T ANY OTHER MUSIC. COOL MUSIC WASN'T INVENTED YET OR SOMETHING. HUH-HUH.

AND UMM, IT'S, LIKE, I WAS WATCHING THIS TV SHOW ABOUT THE BEATLES AND THEY SHOWED AN OLD BEATLES CONCERT AND THE AUDIENCE WAS THE UGLIEST BUNCH OF PEOPLE I'VE EVER SEEN IN MY LIFE. HEH-HEH! AND ALL THESE CHICKS WERE SCREAMING IN PAIN AND HOLDING THEIR HEADS. I FELT SORRY FOR THEM.

THEN THEY SHOWED HOW THE BEATLES WERE ALWAYS RUNNING AWAY FROM ALL THESE HORNY CHICKS. HEH-HEH-HEH! STUPID BUTT-HOLES! IF I WAS IN THE BEATLES AND A CROWD OF HORNY CHICKS WERE RUNNING AT ME, I'D LIKE PUT MY GUITAR DOWN, DROP MY PANTS, AND DO EM ALL, RIGHT THERE ON THE STREET! HEH-HEH-HEH!

HUH-HUH-HUH! ME TOO. UHH, BUT THEN THE BEATLES DIED. HUH-HUH. I THINK PANTERA KILLED THEM.

UMM, I THINK THEY'RE STILL ALIVE, BUTT-HEAD. THEY'RE IN HIDING, CUZ COOL BANDS LIKE PANTERA AND METALLICA SCARED EM OFF. I THINK THEY LIVE IN A CAVE NOW, HEH-HEH-HEH! AND THEY'RE ALL SHAKING AND CRYING LIKE WUSSIES CUZ THEY THINK PANTERA IS GONNA FIND THEM AND KICK THEY'RE ASSES.

OH YEAH! HUH-HUH-HUH. ANYWAY, ALL THESE OLD PEOPLE CALLED "BABY BOOMERS" KEEP BUYING BEATLES STUFF CUZ IT PROBABLY MAKES EM FEEL YOUNG, HUH-HUH-HUH! EVEN THOUGH THEY'RE OLD AND THEY'RE ALL GONNA DIE SOON. HUH-HUH-HUH! BABY BOOMERS SUCK!

ALIEN

THIS MOVIE WAS REALLY COOL, BUT, UMM, THERE WAS ONE SCENE THAT I COULDA DONE A LOT BETTER. HEH-HEH!

AGGGH! THIS FACE-SUCKER THING'S SUCKING MY FACE! AGGGH!

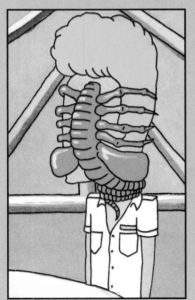

UMM...WAIT A MINUTE.

YEAH. HEH-HEH-HEH! THAT'S BETTER! HEH-HEH-HEH-HEH! YEAH!

DEJA POO

Did you ever go somewhere, and all of a sudden, like, get this funny feeling that one time you took a dump there? It's called Deja Poo. Heh-heh-heh. And it happens to me all the time! Heh-heh! So, like, here's a bunch of places where I felt Deja Poo. Heh-heh-heh! Poop!

NEAR-DEATH EXPEERIENCES: AN EXPEARMINT

UMM, PEOPLE ON TV KEEP TALKING ABOUT PEOPLE WHO, LIKE, DIE. HEH-HEH-HEH. THEN THEY'RE DEAD. HEH-HEH-HMM-HEH.

THAT'S NOT IT, DUMBASS. IT'S LIKE, THEY'RE DEAD, BUT THEY COME BACK TO LIFE. AND THEN THEY TELL EVERYONE ABOUT ALL THE CRAP THEY SAW WHEN THEY WERE DEAD. HUH-HUH-HUH.

OHHH, YEAH. SO, UMM, ME AND BUTTHEAD WANTED TO HAVE ONE OF THESE NEAR DEATH, UMM, EXPEERIENCES AND, LIKE, TELL EVERYONE WHAT IT WAS LIKE. HEH-HEH.

SO, UHH, THE FIRST THING ME AND BEAVIS HAD TO DO WAS DIE. WE THOUGHT IT'D BE COOL IF TODD, LIKE, KICKED OUR ASSES TO DEATH, HUH-HUH-HUH. SO WE WENT UP TO TODD AND LOOKED AT HIM WHILE HE WAS MAKING OUT WITH HIS CHICK, HUH-HUH-HUH.

THEN TODD BEAT THE LIVING CRAP OUT OF US.

THEN WE WERE DEAD, HEH-HEH, "CUZ, UMM, I SAW THIS BRIGHT LIGHT! HEH-HEH.
YEAH, ME TOO. HUH-HUH-HUH. AND, UHH, I REMEMBER I WAS, LIKE, FLYING ABOVE EVERYTHING. HUH-HUH-HUH. I, LIKE, LOOKED DOWN AND SAW YOU ON THE GROUND, BEAVIS. IT WAS COOL!

PLANET OF THE APES

BEAVIS IS SUCH A BUTT-MONKEY, THAT HE WOULD'VE BEEN REALLY GOOD IN THIS MOVIE. HUH-HUH! THIS IS PROBABLY WHAT IT'D BE LIKE IF HE PLAYED THAT ONE HUMAN DUDE:

WHY BEAVIS CAN'T SCORE

IT'S LIKE, A SCIENTIFIC FACT, OR SOMETHING, THAT THERE'S NO WAY BEAVIS WILL EVER SCORE. NO MATTER WHAT. UHH, HERE'S SOME REASONS WHY:

JUST LOOK AT HIM. HUH-HUH-HUH-HUH!

HIS VOICE SOUNDS LIKE AN OLD MAN TRYING TO TALK WHILE HE'S TAKING A MASSIVE DUMP.

CHICKS LIKE TATTOOS. SO ONE TIME, BEAVIS TRIED DRAWING A TATTOO ON HIS ARM. HE, LIKE, TOOK A CRAYON AND DREW A NAD ON HIS ARM. THEN HE WALKED UP TO A CHICK AND SHOWED IT TO HER, BUT IT WAS ALL SMEARED AND SHE COULDN'T TELL WHAT IT WAS. HUH-HUH-HUH!

HIS JAW IS ALL STUCK OUT AND UGLY. IT'S, LIKE, HIS FACE LOOKS LIKE AN EEL. HUH-HUH-HUH! A DORKY EEL.

WE SAW ON TV THAT REALLY RICH DUDES BURN MONEY TO SHOW CHICKS THEY'RE RICH. SO ONE TIME, BEAVIS WALKED UP TO A CHICK AND TRIED DOING THAT WITH A QUARTER. BUT IT GOT REAL HOT AND HE DROPPED IT AND STARTED CRYING.

PLUS, BEAVIS DOESN'T KNOW HOW TO TALK TO CHICKS. THESE ARE SOME OF HIS PICK-UP LINES:

"UMM, HEH-HEH-HEH-HEH-HEH!"

"HEH-HEH-HMM-HEH!"

"HMM-HEH-HEH-HEH! UMMM."

"I GOT A STIFFY, HEH-HEH-HEH!"

"HEH-HEH-HEH-HEH! HEH-HEH!"

"POOP."

EVEN IF A CHICK WANTED TO DO IT WITH BEAVIS, HE PROBABLY WOULDN'T KNOW HOW. HUH-HUH. CUZ HE'S STUPID. TO PROVE HOW STUPID HE IS, I STUCK BEAVIS' HEAD UNDER A MICROSCOPE THING IN CLASS, TO LOOK AT HIS BRAIN. AND HIS BRAIN IS SO SMALL, I COULDN'T EVEN SEE IT. HUH-HUH.

2001: A SPACE ODDITY

THIS MOVIE SUCKS. IT'S, LIKE, THE WORST PIECE OF CRAP EVER. IT WAS, LIKE, THERE WAS A BUNCH OF MONKEYS BEATING EACH OTHER ON THE HEAD, AND THAT WAS COOL, BUT THEN THIS ONE MONKEY THREW THIS BONE INTO OUTER SPACE AND IT TURNED INTO A SPACE SHIP. IT'S, LIKE, WHAT THE HELL IS THAT?! ARE WE SUPPOSED TO BELIEVE THAT'S HOW SPACESHIPS WERE MADE?

THEN ALL THIS SUCKY JAZZ MUSIC OR SOMETHING STARTED PLAYING. THEN SOME DUDES ON A SPACESHIP WERE TALKING TO SOME GUY NAMED HAL WHO WAS HIDING BEHIND A WALL. THEN THERE WAS A BUNCH OF COLORS AND SOME OLD DUDE WOKE UP IN BED AND SAW THIS GIANT CANDY BAR AND HE GOT ALL SCARED OF IT AND DIED. HUH-HUH-HUH. IT SUCKED.

YEAH, REALLY. IT'S, LIKE, IF I WOKE UP AND SAW A GIANT CANDY BAR FLOATING IN MY ROOM, I'D START EATING IT. HEH-HEH-HEH!

MOVIES LIKE THIS JUST PISS ME OFF. UHH, I GUESS THE POINT OF THE MOVIE WAS THAT YOU CAN JUST THROW TOGETHER A BUNCH OF CRAP THAT DOESN'T MEAN ANYTHING AND DOESN'T MAKE ANY SENSE, BUT STUPID PEOPLE LIKE SISKEL AND EBERT WILL SAY "TWO THUMBS UP!" HUH-HUH. I'D LIKE TO GIVE THEM TWO THUMBS UP THE BUTT! HUH-HUH! STUPID PEOPLE THINK THEY KNOW WHAT ALL THAT CRAP MEANS AND THEY'RE ALL SERIOUS AND TALK ABOUT IT, BUT THE GUY WHO MADE THE MOVIE DOESN'T EVEN KNOW WHAT THE HELL IT MEANS. HUH-HUH-HUH!

FROZEN DEAD PEOPLE

SOME REALLY RICH DEAD PEOPLE PAY SCIENCE DUDES, LIKE, 25 THOUSAND DOLLARS TO GET THEIR WHOLE BODY FROZEN SO THAT IN THE FUTURE, SOME OTHER SCIENCE DUDE CAN UNMELT THEM AND BRING THEM BACK TO LIFE. ME AND BEAVIS AREN'T RICH OR DEAD, BUT WE THOUGHT IT'D BE PRETTY COOL TO SEE WHAT THE FUTURE WOULD BE LIKE IN 10 YEARS, SO WE TRIED TO GET FROZEN TOO. HUH-HUH. IT WAS WORKING PRETTY GOOD, BUT THEN THE GUY AT MAXI MART TOLD US TO GET THE HELL OUT OF HIS ICE MACHINE BEFORE HE CALLED THE COPS. HUH-HUH. ASSWIPE.

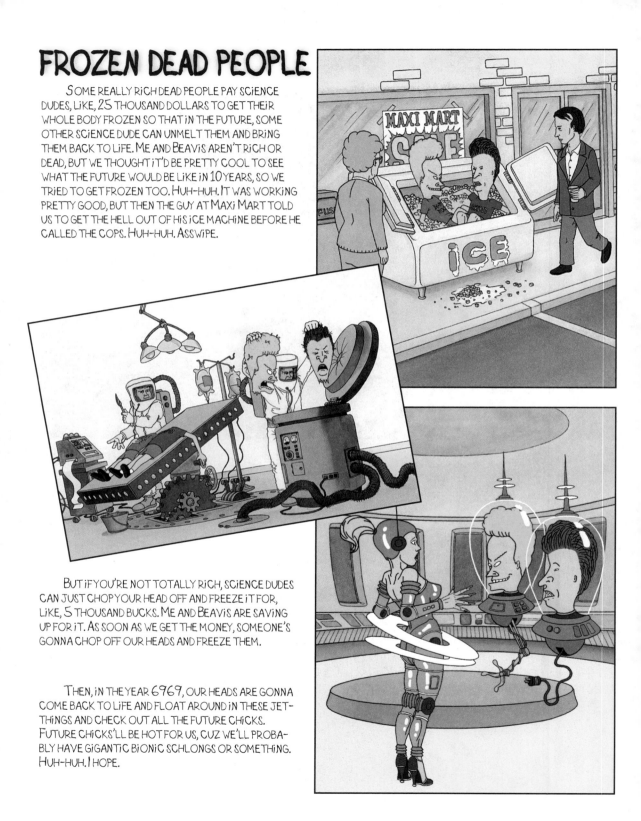

BUT IF YOU'RE NOT TOTALLY RICH, SCIENCE DUDES CAN JUST CHOP YOUR HEAD OFF AND FREEZE IT FOR, LIKE, 5 THOUSAND BUCKS. ME AND BEAVIS ARE SAVING UP FOR IT. AS SOON AS WE GET THE MONEY, SOMEONE'S GONNA CHOP OFF OUR HEADS AND FREEZE THEM.

THEN, IN THE YEAR 6969, OUR HEADS ARE GONNA COME BACK TO LIFE AND FLOAT AROUND IN THESE JET-THINGS AND CHECK OUT ALL THE FUTURE CHICKS. FUTURE CHICKS'LL BE HOT FOR US, CUZ WE'LL PROBABLY HAVE GIGANTIC BIONIC SCHLONGS OR SOMETHING. HUH-HUH. I HOPE.

BLADE RUNNER

Umm, this movie is about this guy that would, like, run around the house with scissors, and his mom's like "stop running with scissors!" Heh-heh-heh! Get it, heh-heh! Blade Runner?

Beavis, you butt-dumpling. Just shut up. His job was to figure out who's a robot and who wasn't and then shoot everybody. If I was that Blade Runner dude and I wanted to tell if someone's a robot, I'd like, wait for them to take a dump. Huh-huh. Then when they're done, I'd go in and check the toilet. If there's just a bunch of screws and nuts and bolts floating in the toilet, that means that person's a robot. Huh-huh.

In the movie, they also had these robots that were, uh-huh-huh, pleasure units. These are robot chicks that you can score with.

Really? Heh-heh! Who'd wanna score with a chick that's like, made of plastic and her boobs are fake and her hair isn't real?

Yeah, really. Huh-huh. I like real chicks like Pamela Anderson and Anna Nicole Smith and Jenny McCarthy.

Yeah, me too. Heh-heh-heh!

SUPERMARKET TABLOIDS

Like, the only reason to learn how to read is to check out those cool newspapers at the register in supermarkets and stuff. Heh-heh! They always got cool stories about cool suppernatural stuff and celebrity people. Me and Butt-Head found a bunch of pictures in the garbage and made our own supermarket tabloid. Cuz, umm, I think that's how they really do it. Heh-heh-heh! Check it out:

Was Elvis Ever Really Alive?

THE DAILY SPANK

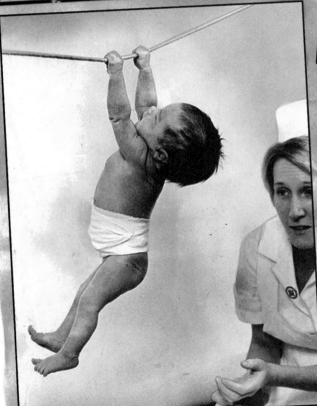

BABY TRIES DARING ESCAPE FROM HOSPITAL!

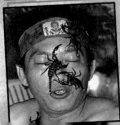

Kitchen Conditions Improving At Burger World

PJ HARVEY AND BILLY CORGAN SEEN LEAVING TRENDY NIGHTCLUB TOGETHER

DOG GROWS FROM DUDE'S HEAD

THE DAILY SPANK

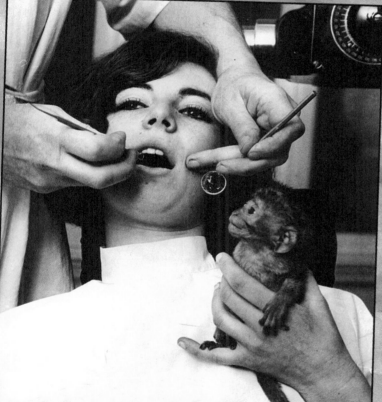

WOMAN SPANKS DENTIST'S MONKEY WHILE HE FILLS HER CAVITY!

ACTRESS SANDRA BERNHARD WEDS!

Dude Chokes His Chicken 500 Times In One Day; Breaks World Record (And Weiner). Says: "Whew! I'm Beat!"

WHY BUTT-HEAD SUCKS

WHY BUTT-HEAD SUCKS. BY BEAVIS. HEH-HEH-HEH! THIS IS GONNA BE COOL! UMM, IT'S, LIKE, A MYSTERY WHY HE SUCKS SO MUCH. FOR AS LONG AS I'VE KNOWN HIM, PEOPLE HAVE BEEN, LIKE, "WHY DOES BUTT-HEAD SUCK SO MUCH?" UMM, I'M HERE TODAY TO TELL YOU WHY:

WHAT THE HELL'S WITH BUTT-HEAD'S GUMS? HEH-HEH-HEH! THEY'RE DISGUSTING! I THINK WHEN HE WAS A LITTLE KID, A DOG RIPPED OFF HIS TOP LIP AND IT NEVER GREW BACK.

HE ALWAYS WEARS THE SAME CLOTHES. I SWEAR IT'S, LIKE, HE ONLY OWNS ONE SHIRT.

PLUS, HIS BREATH STINKS CUZ HE'S ALWAYS GOT FOOD AND CRAP STUCK IN HIS BRACES. AND HIS BRACES ARE ALL RUSTED AND THEY'VE BEEN ON FOREVER.

HIS EYES ARE ALL CROOKED AND STU-PID. UMM, I THINK THAT'S CUZ WHEN WE WERE LITTLE, I HIT HIM IN THE BACK OF THE HEAD WITH A SHOVEL.

HE THINKS HE'S, UM, SMARTER THAN, UM, ME. OR SOMETHING. I DON'T KNOW. MAYBE. UM, WHAT?

ONCE, I PUT THIS BRICK IN MY UNDERWEAR SO WHEN BUTT-HEAD WOULD KICK ME IN THE NADS, HE'D BREAK HIS FOOT, HEH-HEH. BUT LIKE, THAT DAY HE DIDN'T KICK ME! I WALKED AROUND FUNNY ALL DAY WITH THIS BRICK HANGING THERE BETWEEN MY LEGS, SCRATCHING UP MY NUT-SACK. HEH-HEH. SO FINALLY I WAS LIKE, " SO, UMM, BUTT-HEAD. YOU WANNA KICK ME IN THE NADS?" AND HE WAS, LIKE, "UHH, OKAY." BUT JUST THEN MY UNDERWEAR RIPPED AND THE BRICK FELL OUT AND SMASHED MY FOOT. I WAS SCREAMING AND HE KICKED ME IN THE NADS. THE END. HEH-HEH-HEH!

WHEN WE WERE LITTLE, HE USED TO SIT ON MY HEAD ALL THE TIME AND CUT THE CHEESE. AND, UMM, NOW I'M DEAF IN ONE EAR.

OH YEAH, AND HE WANTS TO DO IT WITH MY MOM.

SPACE TRAVEL

Every year, some dumbass predicts that normal people like you and me will be able to travel in outer space someday. Like, we'll be able to drive cars to the moon and check it out. Or maybe ride our bikes to the sun or something. But that's stupid, cuz there isn't any air in space, and everyone would die.

STAR WARS

The *Star Wars* movies all kicked ass. Huh-huh. Darth Vader ruled, but he would've been even cooler if I played him. And Luke Skywalker was a wussy, but if Beavis played him he'd be even more of a wuss. He'd probably be called Luke Fartknocker. Huh-huh-huh!

UHH, WE HEARD THAT IN THE FUTURE, WHEN THAT LUCAS DUDE GETS OFF HIS LAZY ASS, THERE'S GONNA BE THIS NEW MOVIE ABOUT THE DUDES FROM *STAR WARS*. EXCEPT, LIKE, EVERYTHING IN IT'S SUPPOSED TO HAPPEN BEFORE THE FIRST *STAR WARS* MOVIE OR SOMETHING. IT'LL PROBABLY BE LIKE THIS:

SUPPERNATURAL DUDES

Gibby Haynes

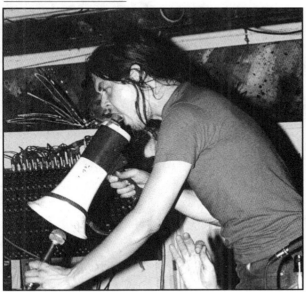

THIS DUDE KICKS ASS! HE'S THE SINGER GUY IN THE BUTTHOLE SURFERS. THEY RULE! HE'S SUPPERNATURAL, CUZ THERE IS NONE COOLER. HE IS THE GREATEST SINGER EVER. LIKE, A LOT OF PEOPLE DON'T KNOW IT, BUT, UHH, ALL THAT IS COOL IN THE WORLD COMES FROM GIBBY. HUH-HUH.

YEAH, REALLY! IT'S, LIKE, IF I WAS A MUSIC DUDE I'D BE JUST LIKE GIBBY. HE'S ALWAYS ALL MESSED-UP AND HE'S, LIKE, 10 FEET TALL AND HE SCREAMS A LOT. HEH-HEH! YOU KNOW, UMM, THERE SHOULD BE A HOLIDAY CALLED BUTTHOLE SURFERS DAY. LIKE, ALL THE KIDS WOULD DRESS UP LIKE GIBBY. THEY'D GLUE ON THESE BAD MOUSTACHES AND MESS UP THEIR HAIR AND TAKE OFF THEIR SHIRTS AND THROW CRAP AND PUKE AND BLOOD ON THEMSELVES. HEH-HEH! THEN THEY'D RUN AROUND RINGING PEOPLE'S DOOR-BELLS AND WHEN SOMEONE COMES TO THE DOOR, THE KIDS WOULD, LIKE, TURN AROUND AND PULL DOWN THEIR PANTS AND SCREAM "HAPPY BUTTHOLE DAY!" HEH-HEH-HEH-HEH!

That Guy On Weather Channel

THIS GUY IS PRETTY DAMN AMAZING. HE MUST BE SUPPERNATURAL CUZ HE KNOWS WHAT IT'S GONNA BE LIKE OUT-SIDE THE NEXT DAY. HUH-HUH. IT'S, LIKE, I WAS WATCHING WEATHER CHANNEL AND I SAW HIM DO IT. HE WAS, LIKE, "UHH, THERE'S GONNA BE RAIN TOMORROW." I WAS, LIKE, "UHH, OKAY, DUDE." BUT, LIKE, THE NEXT DAY, IT WAS RAINING! HUH-HUH-HUH. I WAS, LIKE, "WHOA! THAT'S COOL!"

YEAH! HEH-HEH! WE SAW HIM AT THE MALL. AND, UMM, I GOT HIS AUTO-GRAPH. HEH-HEH-HEH. I WAS LIKE, "HEY, MAN. HOW'S IT GOIN'? SO, WHAT'S IT GONNA BE LIKE TOMORROW?" AND HE WAS, LIKE, "PROBABLY HOT AND SUNNY." AND, LIKE, THE NEXT DAY IT WAS ALL HOT AND SUNNY! I COULDN'T BELIEVE IT! HEH-HEH-HEH! THIS GUY PROBABLY SCORES CONSTANTLY! YOU KNOW, UMM, THE WAY THIS GUY DOES IT, IS HE TIME TRAVELS TO TOMORROW AND THEN HE LOOKS AROUND AND SEES WHAT THE WEATHER'S LIKE. THEN HE GOES BACK AND TELLS EVERYONE! HEH-HEH! SEE, CUZ HOW ELSE COULD HE KNOW THE WEATHER TOMORROW? HEH-HEH!

OH, YEAH. THAT'S COOL!

UHH, OUR CITY IS CALLED BIG CRACK. UH-HUH-HUH-HUH!

THERE'S THIS GIANT GLASS BUBBLE COVERING THE CITY. I DON'T KNOW WHY, BUT THAT'S WHAT ALL FUTURE CITIES HAVE. PROBABLY SO YOU HAVE SOMETHING TO THROW ROCKS AT WHEN YOU'RE BORED.

IN OUR CITY THERE'D BE THIS ONE GIGANTIC TV SET, SO LIKE, NO MATTER WHERE YOU ARE IN THE CITY, YOU CAN STILL WATCH TV ALL DAY LONG. HUH-HUH. AND I GET THE REMOTE. HUH-HUH-HUH! AND IF SOMEONE TRIES TO CHANGE THE CHANNEL THEY GET KICKED IN THE NADS BY MY SECRET SERVICE DUDES.

ALL THE BUILDINGS WILL LOOK LIKE BUTTS AND BOOBS AND WEINERS. HEH-HEH-HEH-HEH-HEH! AND THE ENTRANCES TO THE UNDER-GROUND SUBWAY THINGS WOULD BE SHAPED LIKE, HEH-HEH-HEH-HEH. YOU KNOW. HEH-HEH-HEH!

THERE WILL BE BARE-ASS NAKED CHICKS LAY-ING AROUND EVERYWHERE, READY TO DO IT WITH MY ROYAL SCHLONG.

THE ONLY MUSEUM WOULD BE "THE BEAVIS MUSEUM OF BUTT PORN."

I'D HAVE A COPY OF HIGHLAND HIGH BUILT, HEH-HEH-HEH, THEN I'D GO IN THERE AND WRECK EVERY-THING. THEN I'D TELL THEM TO BUILD IT AGAIN AND I'D WRECK IT OVER AND OVER, HEH-HEH!

THERE'LL BE THIS GIANT TOILET IN THE MIDDLE OF THE CITY, AND IF YOU SUCK, YOU'LL BE THROWN IN THERE AND GET FLUSHED.

STAR TREK: THE NEXT GENERASHUN

THAT DUDE THAT PLAYS CAPTAIN PICCARD IS OLD. HUH-HUH-HUH. WHEN HE DIES, I'LL BET THEY GET ME TO PLAY CAPTAIN PICCARD. HUH-HUH-HUH! PICK HARD. HUH-HUH-HUH! WHEN I TAKE OVER, IT'LL BE LIKE THIS:

'CAPTAIN'S LOG. NUMBER TWO HAS BEEN TELEPORTED TO THE PLANET OF LONELY HOT CHICKS. MAYBE HE'LL FINALLY SCORE. HUH-HUH.

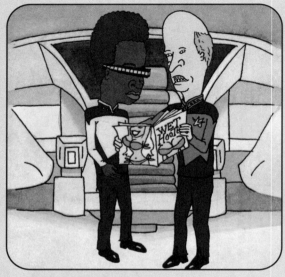

WHOA! HEY, JORDY. CHECK OUT THIS CHICK, HUH-HUH-HUH! UHH...WHAT THE HELL'S WRONG WITH YOU, DUDE? DON'T YOU LIKE CHICKS?

DAMMIT, HOW THE HELL DO YOU TURN ON THE TV? HUH-HUH. UH, LIKE, MAKE IT SO, OR SOMETHING

WHOA! IT'S NUMBER TWO. HUH-HUH-HUH! HEY! HEY, WHAT THE HELL'S GOING ON?! I DIDN'T ASK TO BE BEAMED UP YET! DAMMIT, I WAS ABOUT TO SCORE WITH 40 CHICKS! NOOOO!

TIME TRAVEL

In the future, people will be able to get in time machines and go back in time. Then they can like, change stuff in the past, so that, umm, in the present, things become different and stuff. So like, in a dozen years or something, me and Butt-Head are gonna go back in time to when someone first invented clothes for chicks. Heh-heh.

We'd kick his ass! Heh-heh! That way, clothes for chicks would never be invented! Heh-heh-heh! And all chicks would still be running around naked! Heh-heh. Thank you very much.

VAN DREISSEN SAID THAT IN THE FUTURE WHEN THERE'S TIME MACHINES, TEACHERS ARE GONNA TAKE US BACK IN TIME TO TEACH US ABOUT HISTORY AND STUFF. WHAT A DUMBASS. IF I WANTED TO LEARN ABOUT HISTORY, I'D WATCH THE HISTORY CHANNEL.

BY THE MIRACLE OF TIME TRAVEL, WE'RE HERE AT THE DAWN OF TIME, TO WITNESS THE MOST IMPORTANT MOMENT IN HISTORY. AS THIS ONE BRAVE CREATURE CRAWLS FORTH FROM THE OCEAN, IT IS THE MOMENT WHEN LIFE ON EARTH TRULY BEGINS. IT'S ANCESTORS WILL DEVELOP OVER THE NEXT MIL-LIONS OF YEARS, EVENTUALLY EVOLVING INTO HUMAN BEINGS.

I...I'M MOVED TO TEARS BY THIS WONDEROUS SIGHT. UHH, WHAT THE HELL'S HE TALKING ABOUT? HUH-HUH. WHOA, CHECK IT OUT! HEH-HEH! IT'S SOME LITTLE FISH THING!

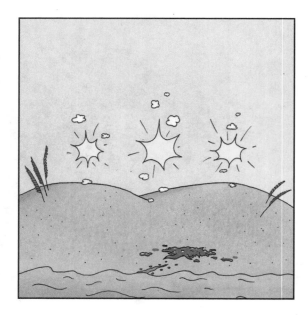

NO! STOP! IF YOU KILL IT, HUMANS WILL NEVER HAVE EVOLVED AND